TEMPLE IN SOCIETY

edited by
Michael V. Fox

Eisenbrauns
Winona Lake
1988

Library of Congress Cataloging-in-Publication Data
Temple in Society.
   Includes bibliographies.
   1. Temples—Comparative studies. I. Fox, Michael V., 1940–.
BL586.T465   1988   291.3′5   88-3979
ISBN 0-931464-38-2

Contents

Preface

Michael V. Fox

The institutions we call temples are found in numerous cultures from widely different times and places—from the dawn of history in Sumer to modern Japan, from the Far East to the Near East, Europe, and Mesoamerica. But are these indeed a single type of institution meeting certain common needs, or are they actually incomparable formations related by little more than a single label? The essays in this volume do not solve this problem, but they do provide a basis to begin answering it—by looking at the essential functions of temples in several disparate societies.

In my view, the temples in Mesopotamia, Egypt, Israel, and many of those in Greece were unmistakably the same kind of institution. Many of them were built on the same architectural principles, employed the same types of personnel, housed similar ritual functions, and expressed the same conceptual principle: the temple is the god's dwelling, or is spoken of as such. Moreover, the Indian temple, as described in Professor Fuller's article, would in my view be at home in the Near East as well (but see the demurral in n. 4 of his article).

Recognizing obvious structural similarities among these institutions does not, however, require us to ignore the equally obvious differences in valuation and function of temples within specific cultural contexts. The distinctive nature of Japanese temples is a salutary reminder of the variety of the institutions called temples. Nevertheless, I believe we are justified in thinking of the temple in its Near Eastern model as a single type of institution whose social functions differ, sometimes radically, from culture to culture. Some of these differences come to light and are put in perspective in the following papers.

The Burdick-Vary Symposium of 1986, held at the University of Wisconsin-Madison, focused on the topic of the role of temples in a few major cultures. The constraints of the symposium made it impossible to include scholars of other major cultures, such as Northern Europe and China. The Egyptologist scheduled to speak, Professor

Klaus Baer (now deceased), was unable to attend. The proceedings therefore sample, rather than survey, the subject. The essays in this volume are reworked versions of the papers presented in symposium, except for the concluding essay by David Knipe, which responds to the other papers and integrates the discussion.

The Symposium was sponsored by the Department of Hebrew and Semitics together with the Institute for Research in the Humanities at the University of Wisconsin in Madison. The Institute is dedicated to the promotion of advanced scholarship in the humanities and offers research fellowships to faculty members of the UW system and to visiting scholars. The participants were:

Walter Burkert
 Professor of Classics
 University of Zürich

Winston Davis
 Wilson-Craven Professor of Religion
 Southwestern University, Georgetown, Texas

Gary M. Feinman
 Associate Professor of Anthropology
 University of Wisconsin–Madison

Michael V. Fox
 Symposium organizer and editor
 Professor of Hebrew and Semitic Studies
 University of Wisconsin–Madison

Christopher J. Fuller
 Lecturer in Anthropology
 London School of Economics

Menahem Haran
 Yehezkel Kaufmann Professor of Bible
 Hebrew University of Jerusalem

David M. Knipe
 Professor of Southeast Asian Studies
 University of Wisconsin–Madison

Samuel Noah Kramer
 Clark Research Professor of Assyriology, Emeritus
 University of Pennsylvania

The Temple in Sumerian Literature

SAMUEL NOAH KRAMER

THE TEMPLE WAS THE LARGEST, tallest, most impressive building in any Sumerian city, which is not surprising in a society whose theologians propounded the dogma from earliest times that the entire city belonged to its principal tutelary deity to whom it had been assigned on the day the world was created. Much is known about the temple's physical features and furnishings from the numerous temples that have been excavated in Sumer.[1] These excavations have also brought to light several hundred votive inscriptions, primarily by the rulers of Sumer, which are of immense historical importance.[2] But all these finds tell us relatively little about the temple's spiritual significance, about the procedures relating to the building and rebuilding of a temple; about the cult and its priestly personnel; about the role of the temple in Sumerian social life; about its impact on the conduct of both the rulers and the people; about the relationship between the temple and the palace; and about its role in commerce and trade, and sometimes even as a cause of war. At least some of these aspects of the Sumerian temple can be filled in with information gleaned from the Sumerian literary documents: their myths and epic tales, their hymns and lamentations.

This paper will provide a fairly comprehensive, but by no means exhaustive, overview of these informative gleanings; it will restrict itself to the literary documents relating to four of the more important temples of Sumer: (1) The Eninnu of Girsu dedicated to the heroic war-god Ningirsu; (2) The Ekur of Nippur dedicated to Enlil, the leading deity of the pantheon; (3) The E'engurra of Eridu dedicated to Enki, the Sumerian water-god noted for his wisdom; (4) The Eanna of Erech dedicated to Inanna, the goddess of love and war.

---

1. For full details see the pages cited in the Index of the *Cambridge Ancient History*, vol. 1/1 (1970) and 1/2 (1971) *sub* Temple.

2. Cf. Edmond Sollberger and Jean-Robert Kupper, *Inscriptions royales sumeriennes et akkadiennes* (Paris: Cerf, 1971); and Horst Steible and Hermann Behrens, *Die altsumerischen Bau- und Weihinschriften* (Wiesbaden: Steiner, 1982).

The Eninnu

The Eninnu was the main temple of Girsu, one of the three cities of the city-state commonly known as Lagaš, whose ruins were excavated by the French many years ago.[3] The Eninnu was dedicated to the god Ningirsu, worshiped primarily as a heroic deity who fought with the monsters of the *Kur*[4] and thus made possible the introduction of irrigation and agriculture in Sumer. Numerous inscriptions concerned with this temple were uncovered, but by far the longest and most informative are two clay cylinders inscribed with the last two hymns of a group of three, recording the rebuilding of the Eninnu by Gudea, a ruler of Lagaš about 2125 B.C.[5] None of the information about the relevant events is provided in a straightforward, systematic manner; it must be deduced, surmised, and inferred from a hymnal composition that is written in a poetic, allusive, elusive, metaphorical, imaginative style replete with mythological motifs, including ad-hoc dreams and their interpretation, divine actions and speeches that could not possibly have taken place except in the poet's imagination, prayers by Gudea that are imaginary wholly or in large part. This attempt at gleaning some of the events that actually took place in the course of Gudea's rebuilding of the Eninnu should therefore be taken as a pioneering effort that will no doubt be modified, corrected, and amplified in the course of time by Sumerologists who may have a deeper understanding of the contents of these two hymns that are among the most ancient literary masterpieces as yet uncovered.[6]

Sometime during his reign, Gudea, the pious ruler of Lagaš, decided to restore and rebuild Ningirsu's temple, the Eninnu. His principle motive in undertaking this sacred task was his belief that it would assure a bountiful water supply and thus insure the prosperity and well-being of his domain, as may be indirectly deduced from the words of the god himself, as conceived in the imagination of the author of the hymns, which read:

3. For a comprehensive study of this temple and its relative position among the other temples of Lagaš, cf. Adam Falkenstein, *Die Inschriften Gudeas von Lagaš* (Rome: Pontifical Biblical Institute, 1966).

4. For the meaning of Sumerian words not translated in this paper, cf. the Glossary in my *History Begins at Sumer* (Philadelphia: University of Pennsylvania, 1981) 358–66.

5. The dates used in this paper have a margin of error of plus or minus 50 years; the very exact dates found in such books as those cited in the preceding notes reflect primarily the demands of the publishers for precise dating.

6. For a reasonably trustworthy translation of the Gudea Cylinders, for the present, Adam Falkenstein and Wolfram von Soden, *Sumerische und Akkadische Hymnen und Gebete* (Zurich: Artemis, 1953) 137–82.

When on my house, the house foremost in all the lands,
The right arm of Lagaš,
That roars like the Imdugud bird in the heavenly orb,
The Eninnu, my royal house,
Oh faithful shepherd Gudea, you lay a faithful hand for me—
(Then) will I call to heaven for rain,
Overflow will descend to you from heaven,
The people will thrive in overflow.
With the founding of my house, abundance will come,
The large fields will grow high for you,
The canals will flood their banks for you,
In the hillocks to which water rose not,
Water will rise up for you,
Sumer will pour out much oil for you,
Will weigh out much wool for you,
The day you fill up my terrace,
My house—the day you lay a faithful hand on it,
To the mountain where the North Wind dwells,
I, having set my foot,
He of immense strength, the North Wind,
From the mountain, the pure place,
Will blow the wind straight towards you.[7]

Before beginning to execute his holy mission, Gudea consulted astrologers, architects, surveyors, and masons as well as experts in extispicy and omens. Then, after presenting Ningirsu with a magnificent chariot, an arrow-filled quiver, and his beloved lyre, he uttered a prayerful entreaty to him for guidance in the rebuilding of his temple, a prayer to which the god responded favorably in these success-promising words which the poet put in the god's mouth:

(Because) I will have given the breath of life to the people,
One man will do the work of more than two,
During the night the light of the moon will shine forth for you,
During the day ample sunlight will shine forth for you,
The house will be built for you during the day,
It will be raised high for you during the night.
From below, the *ḫalub*-tree, the refreshing(?),
Will be brought up to you.
From above the cedar, the cypress and the *zabalum*-tree,
Will be brought to you with ease,

---

7. Cf. Gudea Cylinder I col. XI spaces 1–23.

From the land of the oak,
Oak-trees will be brought to you,
In the mountain of the *na*-stones, the large *na*-stones of the
    mountain,
Will be cut up into slabs for you.[8]

To create the proper spiritual atmosphere for the building of so
holy a sanctuary, Gudea deemed it advisable and necessary to purify
the people of his city morally, ethically, and ritually, and to beautify it
physically. This sociologically significant behavior on the part of the
ruler that includes his effort to create a climate of peaceful fraternity
and equality in his city, is depicted by the poet in these revealing
words:

The *ensi* instructed his city like one man,
Unites the heart of the Lagašites like the sons of one mother,
He planted trees, tore out thorns,
Ripped out weeds, turned back complaints,
Turned back evil to its house,
Removed the tongue of whip and lash,
Put in its place the wool of the mother sheep.
The mother spoke not against the son,
The son contradicted not his mother,
The slave who did wrong,
His master beat him not on the head,
The slave-girl, the captive(?) who worked mischief,
Her mistress struck her not on the face.
To the *ensi* building the house,
To Gudea, no one brought any complaints,
The *ensi* purified the city, cleansed it with fire,
The unclean, the bully, the *gian* he sent out of the city.[9]

Now it was time to start preparing for the actual construction of
the temple, and this involved as a first step the choosing by appropriate omens of the first symbolic brick and inscribing it with the
god's emblem, a joyous act accompanied by the burning of fragrant
incense. The next step was to procure the vast number of workers and
laborers needed for the task. Gudea therefore imposed a levy on each
of the various districts that comprised his domain, and in addition
obtained the services of workers from the foreign lands: Elam, Susa,

8. Cf. Gudea Cylinder I col. XI space 24–col. XII space 9.
9. Cf. Gudea Cylinder I col. XII space 21–col. XIII space 15.

Magan, and Meluhha. The raw materials necessary for the construction of the temple and its furnishings, and which were well-nigh totally lacking in Lagaš, he obtained from distant lands: copper from Dilmun and Kimaš; cedar, cyprus, and *zabalum* wood from their respective mountains; stone from its mountain; bitumen from Magda; gold, silver, and alabaster from their respective mountains.

Before the construction could start, the plan of the temple was worked out by architects and the ground was carefully surveyed. Gudea himself then kneaded the first brick and placed it in a brickmold, and after removing it from the brickmold, carried it in a basket on his head and placed it in the spot where the temple was to be built—symbolic acts accompanied by sacrifices, prayers, music, and jubilation. Now the foundations were laid, ritually supervised and blessed by the *en* and the *lagar*, the two highest priestly officials of the temple. Finally, the temple walls were constructed on a specially built terrace on which six stone statues were erected—five inscribed with very brief laudatory comments relating to Ningirsu, and one to his spouse Bau.

The finished building had an impressive gate structure and numerous chambers including a high rising *giguna*, a divine dining room, bedrooms for Ningirsu and Bau, a cow barn, a kitchen, a beer house, a chariot-house, a music chamber, a funeral chapel, a stone water-basin, several stairways, and high-rising towers in which pigeons nested and swallows rested. Some of the gates and chambers were adorned with stelae representing the heroic deeds for which Ningirsu was famous.

Once the temple had been built, blessed, and sanctified, it was time to install Ningirsu and his spouse in their sacred dwelling in an impressive cultic procedure accompanied by prayers and sacrifices that required such preparatory acts as the cleansing of the temple floor with high quality oil, the ejection of the workers from the building, and the provision of food for the gods, consisting of honey, oil, wine, milk, dates, and grapes. It also made necessary the establishment of a healthy sanitary environment in the city: the smoothing out of street irregularities, the removing of spittle from the walking paths; the healing of the sick. As for spiritual and moral reforms, Gudea, if the poet is to be believed, created such a utopian harmony in his city that even the beasts of the steppes could lie down together, and the lion, leopard, and serpent could sleep side by side in peace.[10] Only then did Ningirsu enter his temple and Bau her chamber amidst much feasting and banqueting.

10. Cf. Gudea Cylinder II col. IV spaces 13–21.

Following the installation of the two deities, the text records the appointment of numerous minor deities, represented perhaps by their priestly personnel, to attend to all of Ningirsu's needs and wants. It also records the presentation by Gudea of such gifts as Ningirsu's chariot and weapons, as well as precious metals and stones and sundry copper pots and pans—all this probably to pave the way for the important symbolic ritual commonly known as the Sacred Marriage Rite, which was believed to insure prosperity and well-being.

The crowning celebration of the installation of Ningirsu in his temple was a seven day festival in Lagaš during which equality, purity, harmony, and justice prevailed. Or, as the poet portrayed it:

On the day his (Gudea's) king (Ningirsu) entered the house,
For seven days,
The slave girl was the equal of her mistress,
The slave stood side by side with his master,
The unclean had to sleep outside the city,
The mischievous tongue was estranged,
Evil was turned back to its house,
The justice of Ningirsu and Nanše he cared for,
The orphan was not wronged by the rich,
The widow was not wronged by the powerful,
The house that had no male heir—the daughter was its heir,
On that day he made justice shine forth,
He subdued evil and oppression.[11]

The remainder of the text is rather fragmentary; it consists largely of the depiction of a banquet which Gudea arranged for the leading deities of the pantheon during which they blessed Gudea and the Eninnu—this hymnal passage provides a good example of the author's poetic, mythological imagination, but tells virtually nothing of what actually happened.

The Gudea Cylinders were inscribed about 2100 B.C. But there is one Lagaš document dating from a quarter of a millennium earlier, which is historical and legal rather than hymnal in character, that is of immense importance for the theme of this symposium. This is the long known and much discussed Urukagina[12] Reform Text dating from about 2350 B.C., which provides a glimpse of the bitter struggle for power, political and economic, between the temple and the palace.

11. Cf. Gudea Cylinder II col. XVII space 18–col. XVIII space 11.
12. *Urukagina* was the pronunciation of the name current until recently when it was demonstrated by W. G. Lambert ("The Reading of the Name uru.KA.gi.na," *Orientalia* 39 [1970] 419) that the correct reading of the name is Uru'inimgina.

This is not the time or place to go into details (a summation as well as a translation of its contents will be found in my *The Sumerians* [Chicago: University of Chicago, 1963] 79–83 and 317–22).

The Ekur

The Ekur was the most hallowed and revered temple in all of Sumer, since it was the home of Enlil, the leading deity of the Sumerian pantheon throughout Sumer's recorded history. According to a well-nigh perfectly preserved devotional hymn dedicated to Enlil,[13] his city Nippur, and his temple, the Ekur, it was Enlil himself, "the great and mighty lord, supreme in heaven and earth, the all-knowing one who understands judgement," who had set up his seat in the Ekur (known also as Duranki, "Center of the Universe"), made princeship preeminent in its "great place, the *kiur*," and erected his dwelling in Nippur, the city that unites heaven and earth.

Having mentioned Nippur, the poet portrays the city as the fearful guardian of man's moral and spiritual values in eulogistic phraseology and imagistic diction which even if only partially true makes Nippur the most ethically-oriented holy city in the entire ancient Near East. Nippur's face, in the words of the poet, is fearsome awe; its outside no mighty god dare approach; its inside is filled with cries of mutilation and "the mouth of catastrophe"; it is a trap and a pit against the rebellious land; it grants not long life to the arrogant; it allows no evil word to be spoken against judgment; it does not tolerate hypocrisy, distortion, abuse, malice, unseemliness, envy, brute force, libellous speech; it is a city whose arm is a vast net, whose hand the evil and the wicked cannot escape; it is a city endowed with truth, where righteousness and justice are perpetuated; where family life is orderly and dutiful; the older brother honors the younger brother and treats him humanely; the word of the father is heeded; the son humbly fears his mother. It is in this city that Enlil, "the great father," raised his beloved shrine of abundance, the Ekur, in a pure place.

The author now turns from holy Nippur to its hallowed shrine, the Ekur, and sings of the mystery of its divine laws, the *me*, and the enduring nature of its rituals, as conducted by its expert priesthood. Or, as the poet puts it: Its *me* that no one dare gaze upon, like heaven cannot be overturned; its pure rites like earth are eternal; in the Ekur prayers and incantations are recited and favorable omens

13. For the edition of this composition, cf. David Reisman, "Two New Sumerian Royal Hymns" (Diss., University of Pennsylvania, 1969) 41ff.

are pronounced; its rituals are precious; its festivals, overflowing with milk and cream, are alluring of plan and full of rejoicing; its banquets and feasts are celebrated from sunrise to sunset.

To attend to all these rituals, rites, and celebrations, the Ekur, according to the poet, had a distinguished priesthood, including the *en* (high priest) and his associate the *lagar*, as well as the *guda* the lustration priest, and the *mueš* who was proficient in prayers. As for the acquisition of the food offerings and animal sacrifices that accompanied the rites, rituals, and celebrations, the Ekur had no worries on that score, for it was the king himself, designated as the "noble farmer" and "faithful shepherd" of the Land, who brought the necessary provisions in large quantities into the Ekur. What is more, he saw to it that the foreign lands which he had conquered by the grace of Enlil, brought their heavy booty to the Ekur's storehouses. For the Ekur, being the center of the universe, was the "breath of life" and "protective shade" of all the peoples, foreigners as well as Sumerians, so that all the lands bowed their heads to it, and all the lords and princes conducted there their sacrifices, prayers, and orisons.

In addition to this rather long, complex Enlil hymn of which only approximately the first half has been summarized above, there are several rather brief hymns dedicated to the Ekur and to some of the shrines within the Ekur complex that concern Enlil's sons, the gods Nanna and Ninurta, as well as his wife Ninlil, his vizier Nusku, and even his "second" wife Šuzianna. From these we learn something about the Ekur's physical components: it had a "house of darkness that knew no light," perhaps a prison, as well as numerous gates including a "lofty gate," a "gate of peace," a "lofty stairway," a "great gate of judgment," a gate "where no grain was cut," an assembly hall, a plow-kiosk, a high-rise *giguna*, to mention only those whose names are intelligible to some extent.[14]

But contradictory and paradoxical as it may seem, this fearsome, awe-inspiring, hallowed and revered Ekur suffered numerous ravaging attacks and was not infrequently desecrated and defiled. Usually this was the cruel work of Sumer's bitter enemies such as the Elamites, the Subarians, the Gutians, and as yet unidentified Su-people. But there is at least one instance in which the king of the Land himself, the fourth ruler of the dynasty founded by Sargon the Great (about 2300 B.C.) committed these terrible acts against the Ekur. This is the theme of a quasi-historical poetic composition commonly known as "The Curse

---

14. Cf. Åke Sjöberg, *The Collection of the Sumerian Temple Hymns* (Locust Valley, N.Y.: Augustin, 1969); and my "Hymn to the Ekur," *Rivista Degli Studi Orientali*, 32 (1957) 95ff.

of Agade," whose author, searching for the cause of one of Sumer's most humiliating defeats at the hands of the barbarous Gutians, claimed that it was due to Naram-Sin's outrageous desecration of the Ekur in retaliation for Enlil's refusal to come to the aid on his (Naram-Sin's) capital Agade in her days of trouble. Naram-Sin's demolishing of the Ekur is described by the poet in a long simile-laden passage that gives some idea of its physical structure and great wealth: he desecrated and defiled the sacred *giguna*; he broke up the foundations of the Ekur with sharp large axes; he ripped out its drain-pipes and removed its door-frames; he cut grain at the gate "where no grain was cut"; he demolished the gate of peace, and peace vanished from all the lands; he defiled the holy vessels; burnt the innocent, protective *lahama*-statues; carried off its gold, silver, and copper vessels in large boats docked at the side of the temple.[15]

But fortunately, Enlil, according to the poets, made sure that the destruction of his Ekur was followed by its restoration and return to its former glory. Thus there is a hymn dedicated to Ur-Nammu, the founder of the Third Dynasty of Ur (about 2050 B.C.) which portrays him as the king especially chosen by Enlil to restore his Ekur in Nippur. After he had defeated Sumer's foes and the Land once again enjoyed prosperity, its foundations were laid firmly, and its terrace was filled to the accompaniment of songs of exaltation by the *enqum* and *ninqum*. Ur-Nammu then proceeded to adorn the Ekur beautifully and to raise its head sky-high, as the people looked on in wonder; he decorated with electrum and refined silver its numerous gates; re-established the *giguna* in its midst like a lofty tower; beautified fittingly Ninlil's chamber, the Gagišua, where she and her spouse Enlil lived happily together.[16]

Another king who rebuilt and restored the Ekur was the brave and pious fourth ruler of the Isin Dynasty, Išme-Dagan (about 1950 B.C.). In a self-laudatory hymn of considerable length he depicts his devoted service in the Ekur in more specific and concrete terms than is usual in the hymnal compositions. Thus he claims that "after the Flood had raged," that is, after a dire calamity had befallen Sumer, Enlil elected him on a propitious day by oracle, and having looked upon the Ekur with joyful eyes, charged him to attend to the daily needs of the Ekur and of Ninil's shrine the *kiur*, and that he executed this mandate in faithful detail: he gathered together all the *me* of the

15. For the edition of this composition, cf. Jerrold S. Cooper, *The Curse of Agade* (Baltimore: Johns Hopkins University, 1983).

16. For a translation of this composition, cf. Kramer, *ANET*[3] (1969) 583–84, where the relevant bibliographical references can be found.

Ekur; searched and found its ancient master-plan; restored its neglected rites; stationed the gracious *udugs* in the courtyard of the temple; installed the gracious *lamas* in the Ekur; offered up many sacrifices to Enlil, including numerous regular offerings of oxen and sheep; reinstituted challenging contests; showered upon the offerings in the temple wine and beer like rain gushing down from the heaven; turned the Ekur daily into a harvest feast; during the festivities that took place on the seventh and fifteenth day of every month he brought fresh milk and cream, and the first fruit of the palm-groves to Enlil's offering-table, and made the Ekur fragrant with incense like a fragrant cedar forest.[17]

From several of the texts cited earlier it was evident that the Ekur was noted for the fear and terror which it inspired in the people of Sumer and even the foreign lands. But there is one document whose author seems to have concentrated on finding synonymous and alternative words, phrases, and metaphorical expressions to depict this horrifying aspect of the Ekur: the fear, dread, terror, dismay, consternation, and panic which it aroused, especially in the hearts of the evil and the wicked. More importantly, this composition seems to revolve about the themes of guilt and punishment, and it may illuminate some aspects of the actual Sumerian judicial process and penal system, such as the water-ordeal and the use of prisons—there is even some possibility that the Ekur complex included a mournful, sorrowful Nether-World-like chamber for the wretches found guilty after judgment. In any case, here is detailed summation of the contents of this extraordinary hymnal document dedicated to the goddess Nungal who is designated as the "Queen of the Ekur."[18]

The poet begins with a description of the Ekur as a furious storm of the heaven and earth raging against the enemies, as a huge pillory of the universe; its dark chamber terrifies the flesh; it is a raging, high-rising sea; it is a trap that lies in wait for the evil-doer and makes tremble the flesh of the wicked; it is a finely-meshed net that imprisons people; it is a house that examines closely both the righteous and the wicked and does not allow the wicked to escape; it is the divine "River of Ordeal" which, having identified the sinner, does not kill the righteous man; it is a prison which metes out penalties to the guilty.

17. This summary is based on a yet unpublished edition of the composition prepared by Barry Eichler.

18. For an edition of this composition, cf. Åke Sjöberg, "Nungal in the Ekur," *Archiv für Orientforschung* 24 (1973) 19–46, and for its interpretation, cf. Tikva Simone Frymer, "The Nungal Hymn and the Ekur-prison," *Journal of the Economic and Social History of the Orient* 20 (1967) 78–89.

From this portrayal of the house as a whole, especially as a terrifying place of judgment, the poet turns to a depiction of the dreaded aspects of each of its individual, structural components, beginning with the foundations and concluding with the lock and bolt, thus: its foundations are garbed in awe; its gate is blue dusk raising goose-flesh; its doorsill is an open-mouthed dragon lying in wait for a man; its threshold is a "noble" dagger whose sides keep stabbing the evil man; its architrave is a scorpion darting out of the ground; its buttressed *dubla* structure is a lion whom no one dares attack; its vault is a rainbow garbed in awesome fear; its hinge is an eagle with gripping claws; its door is a big mountain that does not open for the evildoer but does open for the righteous man and does not hold him back; its bolt is a fierce lion; its bar is a snake that sticks out its tongue as it twists and coils; its lock is a viper that slithers about in a fearsome place.

Following a passage of rather uncertain import which introduces Nungal, a mighty deity whose halo covers the universe, as the queen of the Ekur, the goddess is depicted as taking her seat on her dais to judge mankind and as casting her finely-meshed net over the Land so that the wicked cannot escape. Moreover, having caught a young man who did not acknowledge his personal god at the gate of the temple, she made him take the road, blindfolded and naked, to the "house of lament,"—a kind of "hell on earth," where hostility, hatred, discord, and madness predominate, a house filled with nothing but tears, groans, and lament; whose brickwork tears apart the wicked, but grants life to the righteous.

What follows is not very clear. It seems that the prisoner, perhaps after having undergone the misery and torture of the "house of lament," is given another chance, and this time it is the merciful and compassionate side of the goddess that comes to the fore. Thus, according to the poet, there came a day when the gods stationed themselves alongside the divine River of Ordeal that separates the righteous from the wicked, granting life to the just but clamping down on the evildoer so that he cannot escape. On that day Nungal acclaimed and exalted herself by accentuating her distinguished divine ancestry, by delineating some of her powers, but emphasizing the merciful and compassionate aspects of her character, by asserting that she keeps special watch over the Sumerians; that she holds the tablet of life in her hands, and that though she does not let the wicked escape her power, she is a merciful mother who lightens penalties; moreover she calms the stormy evil heart and saves the people from the "mouth of catastrophe," that is, perhaps, from the River of Ordeal.

For we next find the goddess naming several of her divine helpers, including Nindimgul, the divine mooring pole who stretches out her arm and raises the accused out of the "mouth of catastrophe," and brings him into her house of life where presumably she puts him under guard until he soothes the heart of his personal god with tears and laments. Finally she herself purifies and refines him like refined silver, and returns him to the hand of his god who will show his gratitude by praising and exalting her name unto distant days.

The E'engurra

It is quite a relief to leave Enlil's dreaded Ekur with its emphasis on judgment and punishment and turn to Enki, the god of water and wisdom, and his temple in Eridu, known as the E'engurra, the "Seahouse" or as Abzu, the "Watery Deep." In one rather brief hymn dedicated to this temple, there is not a word about fear and terror, evil and guilt. Rather it is depicted as a large, pure, holy, song-filled "banquet hall" where pure food for the gods was prepared in large ovens and pure water was drunk from large bowls.[19] In a myth concerned with Enki's organization of the earth and its cultural processes, the E'engurra is depicted as a house whose shade stretches over the marshes; as a place where fishes frolic and birds chirp; where songs are chanted and spells recited.[20]

A considerably more detailed portrayal of the E'engurra is sketched in a hymn-like myth dedicated to Enki, commonly known as "Enki and Eridu: the Journey of the Water-god to Nippur."[21] In this composition the poet describes the E'engurra symbolically and metaphorically as a luminous cheer-bringing temple built of silver and lapis lazuli and adorned with gold; a house whose very bricks are eloquent and resounding, and whose reed hedges roar like a bull; its foundation is planted in the "Deep"; its lock is unrivalled; its bolt is a fearful noble beast; its roof-beam is an artfully shaped "Bull of Heaven"; its vault is a bull with horns raised; its gate is a noble beast gripping a man; its doorsill is a lion rising up against a man; it is a house by the seaside resounding with sacred incantations and filled with harmonious melodies accompanied by musical instruments. Toward the end of the composition the poet depicts Enki himself

19. Cf. Sjöberg, *Collection of the Sumerian Temple Hymns*, 17–18.

20. For bibliographical reference to this Enki myth, cf. *The Sumerian Dictionary* (ed. Åke Sjöberg; Philadelphia: The University Museum, 1984), B: x, *sub* "Enki and the World Order."

21. For bibliographical reference, cf. ibid., *sub* "Enki's Journey to Nippur."

preparing the food and drink essential for a joyous feast in a scene which, it is not unreasonable to assume, reflects an actual temple preparatory banquet procedure. First he poured beer into large bronze vessels; next he mixed bran-mash of the very best beer with date-syrup; finally he baked the bran-mash into a refreshing honey-bread, and gave it to Enlil to eat in his Nippur shrine.

But despite its purity, its incantations, and its joyous music, the E'engurra, like the awesome Ekur, was ravaged, defiled, demolished, and desecrated from time to time. One such catastrophe took place early in the second millennium and was commemorated in a composition known as a "Lamentation Over the Destruction of Eridu."[22] It is only partially preserved, but from its extant text, which adds relatively little that is relevant to our theme, we learn that one of the E'engurra's component shrines was a "House of Wisdom," dedicated to Nidaba, the patron deity of writing, and that the temple personnel included a priest designated as *lú-naḫ*, literally "noble man," and a priestess designated as *nin-dingir*, literally "lady-divine."

The Eanna

The Eanna of Erech was the temple of the goddess Inanna, the most beloved and one of the most feared deities of the Sumerian pantheon. She was worshiped under three aspects that at least on the surface seem to be unrelated and even antithetical: as the Venus goddess in charge of the bright evening and morning star; as the goddess of war and weaponry who wrought havoc on all who displeased her, but especially upon Sumer's enemies; as the goddess of love and procreation who ensured the fertility of the soil and the fecundity of the womb. She was celebrated in myth, epic, and hymn more than any other deity, male or female,[23] but relatively little that is concrete, specific, and definite is known about her cult. What is known relates primarily to the Sacred Marriage Rite, a rite celebrated during the course of the centuries in various Sumerian cities, but whose place of origin was most probably Erech: it was the theologians of Erech who sometime about 3000 B.C. conceived and developed the rather attractive idea that in order to make the land flourish and prosper, it was the not unpleasant duty of the king to wed Inanna, the

22. Cf. Margaret Green, "Eridu in Sumerian Literature" (Diss., Oriental Institute of the University of Chicago, 1975) 334–65.
23. For fuller details, see my book, *From the Poetry of Sumer* (Berkeley: University of California, 1979) 50–97.

desirable, alluring goddess of love who controlled the productivity of the soil and the fecundity of the womb of both man and beast.[24]

The Erech origin of the Sacred Marriage Rite may be surmised from several epic tales composed about 2000 B.C., or several centuries earlier, which reflect a historical episode that took place much earlier in the third millennium B.C. These epic tales relate in large part to a war between Enmerkar, the *en* of Erech and Ensuḫkešdanna, the *en* of Aratta, an important city in south-central Iran that was renowned for its wealth of precious metals and stones as well as the craftsmen who worked them into attractive, decorative ornamentation. These were the very assets which Erech lacked, and the aggressive Enmerkar decided to declare war on Aratta in order to acquire them, and the excuse he gave was that he needed both the raw materials and the craftsmen to decorate and adorn Inanna's temple. Here then we may have an example of the role of the temple as a cause of war, or at least as a wily justification for a call to arms.[25]

To return to the Sacred Marriage Rite—there are extant quite a number of hymns and chants relating to the courting, wooing, and marriage of the goddess by the deified shepherd-king Dumuzi; they tell us very little about what actually took place during the celebration of the rite, since they include much that is imaginative and fanciful and little that is factual and real. Thus according to one Šulgi hymn, the sexual union between the goddess and Šulgi, conceived as Dumuzi incarnate, took place in the Eanna of Erech whither Šulgi had traveled by boat, and after he had dressed himself in a special ritual garment and covered his head with a crown-like wig.[26] On the other hand, there is a hymn exalting Inanna primarily as the Venus star, which describes the rite as being performed on the eve of New Year's day in the palace of the king Iddin-Dagan, and that step by step this is what took place: First, a bed of rushes and cedar was set up and over it was spread a specially prepared coverlet. Then Inanna was washed and soaped and presumably laid on the bed. The king then proceeded, on ground fragrant with cedar oil, with "lifted head," to the "holy lap" and blissfully bedded with the goddess. The following day a rich banquet was prepared in the large reception hall of the

24. For fuller details, see my book, *The Sacred Marriage Rite* (Bloomington: Indiana University, 1969) 49–66.

25. The three epic tales relating to the war between Erech and Aratta are "Enmerkar and the Lord of Aratta," "Enmerkar and Ensuhkešdanna" (cf. *The Sumerian Dictionary*, B: x), "Lugalbanda Epic II" (cf. ibid., xvi). Some scholars now identify Aratta with the ruins of Shahr-i-Sochte; cf. F. Vallat, *Joint Seminar on Development of Complex Societies of South-West Iran*, 24–29 June 1985, pp. 36ff.

26. For an edition of this Šulgi hymn, see Jacob Klein, *Three Šulgi Hymns* (Ramat Gan: Bar-Ilan University, 1981) 124–66.

palace; there was much eating and drinking, music and song, as the people "paraded" before the divine couple sitting side by side on their thrones.[27]

Even assuming that this depiction of the Sacred Marriage Rite is at least partially true, it leaves unanswered such specific questions as whether the ceremonies took place annually or only from time to time, and especially who actually represented the goddess during the celebration. One fact is reasonably certain: the Sacred Marriage Rite was one of the principal components of Inanna's cult and that it was characterized by orgiastic, ecstatic behavior, and probably even by bloody castration, on the part of some of its participants. For among these we find male prostitutes with special beribboned hairdos; hierodules of various categories; men and women carrying sword-belts and spears; devotees who dressed their right side in women's clothing and their left side in men's clothing; dagger-holding *kur-garras*; worshipers who kept sprinkling blood from their blood-covered daggers—to mention only those whose function and behavior are intelligible to some extent.

But despite her universal adoration and the ecstatic worship of her cult devotees, Inanna could not save her temple from destruction and desecration by Sumer's ruthless enemies, and because of her grief and suffering became one of the models of the "weeping goddess" prototypes of the *mater dolorosa*. This is evidenced by the numerous liturgical litany-padded laments composed by the Babylonian poets during the latter part of the first half of the second millennium B.C. which portray the goddess lamenting the loss of her temple in such plaintive words as:

> The bird has its nesting place—my young are dispersed,
> The fish lies in calm waters, but I—my resting place exists not,
> The dog kneels at the threshold but I—I have no threshold,
> The cow has a place to lie down but I—I have no place to lie down,
> The ewe has its fold but I—I have no fold,
> The beasts have a place to sleep but I—I have no place to sleep.[28]

Inanna was not the only "weeping goddess"; there are quite a number of these grieving suffering goddesses who could be so

27. For the edition of this hymn, see Reisman, "Two New Sumerian Royal Hymns," 147ff.

28. For a sketch of the contents of texts relating to the "weeping goddess," see my article, "The Weeping Goddess; Sumerian Prototypes of the *Mater Dolorosa*," *Biblical Archaeologist* 46 (1983) 69–80.

designated. The image of the "weeping goddess" that was first created
by the Sumerian poets following the disastrous destruction of Ur and
its temple about 2000 B.C. no doubt mirrored the bitter despair of the
Sumerians at the sight of their ruined temples that had been so
lovingly built and designed, with such high hope and joyous promise
of divine blessings to ensure the prosperity and well-being of the city,
the land, and the people—and now were no more.[29]

29. There were at least 42 major temples in Sumer, and brief hymns to each were
collected and compiled as one homogenous composition of 545 lines by the Sumerian
scribes who lived in the last quarter of the third millennium B.C. In 1969, Åke Sjöberg
published an edition of this text which is fairly well preserved (cf. nn. 14 and 19
above), but much of whose contents still remain rather obscure and enigmatic; the
same is true of the fully preserved "Keš Temple Hymn" edited by Gene B. Gragg in the
same volume. In 1975 appeared *Le Temple et le Culte* (Compte rendu de la vingtième
Rencontre assyriologique internationale; Leiden: Rencontre assyriologique internationale,
1972), a volume that contains a number of valuable articles on various aspects of the
temple and its cult throughout the ancient Near East. Only one, "Die Einweihung des
Eninnu" by H. Sauren, is closely related to our theme, but it is so full of unverified and
unverifiable assumptions, conjectures, and interpretations that it can hardly be recommended as a relatively trustworthy scholarly contribution.

Temple and Community in Ancient Israel

MENAHEM HARAN

THE BASIC TERM applied to the temple in biblical Hebrew, *bêt Yahweh* 'the house of the LORD', testifies to the primary character of this institution, as fossilized in linguistic usage. Likewise, the epithet reserved exclusively for priests in biblical diction, 'servants of the LORD', is indicative of the primary comprehension of their role as attendants of the deity in its house. In the course of time these concepts were refined, although the ancient Israelite religion, no more than the religions preceding it, never thought of abandoning the cultic clichés associated with the 'house of God'. From this perspective, the temple is fundamentally different from the synagogue, which is only a gathering place of the community for liturgical purposes and an entirely new institution. With its appearance, Judaism could practically do without the 'house of God' and thus it could absorb the blow of the Second Temple's fall without collapsing. Prayer, however, far from being the creation of the synagogue, was also prevalent in the temple courts, where it was found outside the priestly circle and was not part of the cultic activity proper. There are no grounds for the claim that priests engaged in prayer in the First Temple period. In the Second Temple period, however, prayer was institutionalized in Judaism.

Houses of God and Priesthood

The term "temple" serves in the English translations of the Bible as the equivalent of the Hebrew word *hêkhāl*, which also occurs in Canaanite and is a loanword from Akkadian *êkallu* (which, in turn, stems from the Sumerian *ê-gal*, meaning 'big house'). The combination *hêkhal Yahweh*, 'the palace (or big house) of the Lord', is only one of the epithets attributed to the institution erected by King Solomon in Jerusalem.[1] The fundamental, defining name of that institution is,

---

1. Such as 'lofty house', *bêt zebûl*; '(place of) holiness', *miqdash*; 'house of holiness', *bêt hammiqdash* (only in 2 Chr 36:17); 'the Lord's tent', *'ohel*; 'the Lord's

however, 'the house of the Lord', *bêt Yahweh*, or 'the house of God', *bêt ʾĕlohîm*. The Bible speaks of other "houses of God" besides the two "temples" of Jerusalem (the first, ca. 950–587 B.C.E.; the second, ca. 515 B.C.E.—70 C.E.). These two were preceded by a dozen earlier houses of God erected at various places throughout the country (such as Shiloh, Bethel, Dan, Gilgal in Ephraim, Mizpah in Benjamin, Hebron), some of which originated in the Israelite settlement in Canaan.[2] When Solomon built the First Temple of Jerusalem, some early houses of God had already declined and faded away.

Further, the term 'house of God' clearly designates the institution's primary function, which was exactly what the term implies—a house for the god, his dwelling place. Just as every temporal king, and indeed any man, has his own domicile, so the divine king, in whose shadow the community finds protection, has a residence of his own. And in this dwelling place, just as in every luxurious house, the master of the residence is provided with all his "needs": bread set on the table, incense for smell, lamps for light, meat-, grain-, and drink-offerings presented on the outer altar—the altar which in the fossilized cultic language is still referred to as "the Lord's table" (Ezek 44:16; Mal 1:7). In this dwelling place, moreover, the master of the residence has his own servants, the priests, who care for his necessities and keep the house in order—just as any reigning monarch has in his palace servants and retinue surrounding him constantly and performing his orders.

The priests, being the servants of God, are thus not regarded at all as representatives of the community. Their obligation to fulfil their role in the service of God, that is, to perform the cultic acts, is bestowed on them from birth by divine will and is taken to be their exclusive privilege. This privilege does not stem from the community's authority but is based on the notion that a special "eternal covenant of priesthood" was granted by God to the ancestor of priests, Phinehas son of Eleazar son of Aaron, "to him and his descendants after him" (Num 25:13). This covenant is analogous to the one made with David (2 Sam 7:4–29), in which God promised that David's royal throne "will be established forever" (2 Sam 7:13, 16; cf. Ps 89:4–5; 132:11–12). The fact that the priests are singled out from all other parts and

---

dwelling', *nāweh*. See my book *Temples and Temple-Service in Ancient Israel* (reprinted Winona Lake, Ind.: Eisenbrauns, 1985) 13–15.

2. A complete list of these houses of God is to be found in *Temples and Temple-Service*, 26–42. Houses of God should not be confused with cultic precincts of the open type, a few of which achieved high degrees of prominence, and their foundations were mostly ascribed to the Patriarchs and are reported in the Book of Genesis (*Temples and Temple-Service*, 48–57).

functionaries of society is indicated by the epithet reserved exclusively for them in the biblical diction: "servants [or attendants] of the Lord," "servants of God" (Isa 61:6; Jer 33:21–22; Joel 1:9, 13, et al.). They are also depicted as "standing before the Lord to serve him" (Deut 10:8; 17:12; 18:5, 7, et al.), "drawing near to the Lord to serve him" (Ezek 40:46; 43:19; 44:15), "drawing unto his table to serve him" (Ezek 44:16), in all of which cases the verb 'to serve', Hebrew *šrt*, is employed.[3] This is not merely a stereotyped phrase, nor solely a metaphor, but an actual expression of the priest's special function, a remnant of a primary historical comprehension of the task as fossilized in linguistic usage.

Incidentally, since the priests' function was conceived of as a matter of high-ranking nobility in the service of God, their role was not only the privilege of special families (in which respect they differed from prophets, whose activity was considered a personal gift of divine grace). The priests' status was regarded as more prestigious than that of prophets. To be sure, over the course of time it has become evident that the writings of the Hebrew Bible prophets (those who are designated "classical" prophets) have preserved some unique compositions, of remarkable literary perfection and a message relevant even to the modern reader living in a semisecular environment. In ancient Israel, however, it was priesthood that, as an essentially sacral and aristocratic phenomenon, ranked above prophecy.[4]

It should be added immediately that, in fact, ancient Israelite religion was long since freed from such a crude comprehension of the nature of God as to depict Him as being in need of the provision of food or incense. Even in the pre-Israelite ancient Near Eastern religions the conception of the divine had already shed such physical limitation. Nonetheless, neither the ancient Israelite religion, nor those that preceded it, ever thought of abandoning the cultic clichés and practices associated with the temple, that is, the house of God,

3. The prophet's conventional epithet is, by contrast, "slave of the Lord" (1 Kgs 14:18; 15:29; 2 Kgs 9:33; 10:10; Isa 20:3, et al.), which is also used as Moses' title (Num 12:7–8; Deut 34:5; Josh 1:1–2, et al.). Prophets in general are referred to as "my slaves the prophets," "his slaves the prophets," where the inflected Hebrew noun for "slaves" is directed to God (2 Kgs 9:7; 17:13, 23; Jer 7:25; 25:4, et al.). This epithet, which probably originated in prophetic circles is also projected upon other figures, such as Abraham (Gen 26:24; cf. 20:7), David (2 Sam 7:5, 8; 1 Kgs 8:66, et al.), Job (Job 1:8; 2:3; 42:7–8).

4. This fact is reflected, among other things, in the usage of the biblical language, where the rule is that whenever the two are mentioned together, the priest comes first (1 Kgs 1:32–38; Isa 28:7; Jer 4:9, et al.). In Jer 6:13; 8:10, the order has been reversed, but the prophet still corresponds here to "the least of them" and the priest to "the greatest of them." Thus, the relative rank of each one of the two is retained.

even though the institution itself had certainly emerged in a most distant past, at a time when man first started conceiving of the divine forces as possessing personal and distinct character. To put it differently, it was not the ancient Israelite religion that invented the house of God; this institution came to it ready-made, with its identifying marks clearly discernible.[5] It is a good general rule that all religions in history do not usually create their institutions *ex nihilo*, but inherit them from earlier stages and mostly only infuse them with a new spirit or afford them a special meaning. After all, the modes of worship associated with the house of God are not much more anthropomorphic than the practice of prayer, which itself is also an inheritance from the hoary past.

Thus, the notion that the temple is constitutionally a house of God and the priest is his servant was virtually a cornerstone in the ancient Israelite and the ancient Near Eastern conception of the world, so that the prophets, too, could only share in it. From this perspective there was no real contrast between priest and prophet, for one did not mean to take the other's place nor did one deny the substantiality and the validity of the other: just as the priest was acknowledged as the servant of God, so the prophet was recognized as the one who makes known the word of God (unless he was considered a "false" prophet). If the prophets sometimes engaged in bitter controversy against the priests, this is only an expression of their antagonism to the social establishment and should by no means be construed as denial of the functional validity of the servants of God nor as a rejection of the indispensability of priests in an orderly society. For in prophecies of consolation they do not refrain from exalting the Lord's servants and envisage Israel's restoration as a reinstitution of the temple service no less than as a renewal of the Davidic kingdom. In Second Isaiah's glowing vision, "all the flocks of Kedar" and "the rams of Nebaioth" shall be assembled in the time of Israel's redemption in order to "come up" on the altar (Isa 60:7). This attitude never disappeared. In the Jewish prayer book, the plea for restoring worship to the temple and reinstating the priests in their service is still one of the central expressions of eschatological expectation.

5. Therefore, it is rather inaccurate to state, as some historians used to do, that the Jews, having had a genius for organizing their religious life invented two central institutions, Temple and Synagogue. For the former was inherited from previous historical stages (while the latter really is a Jewish creation; see further). For the comprehension of the temple as a divine dwelling place in ancient Near Eastern religions, see the series of articles by H. H. Nelson, A. L. Oppenheim, G. E. Wright, and F. V. Filson under the general titles "The Significance of the Temple in the Ancient Near East," *Biblical Archaeologist* 7 (1944) 44, 58–59, 66–68.

Synagogue and Prayer

In order to perceive properly the nature of the temple, it is worthwhile to point out its fundamental difference from the synagogue. The synagogue is basically a gathering place of the community for liturgical purposes—viz., for public prayer (like any religious experience, prayer is also preferably a communal matter, even though it may be performed by individuals). The synagogue is not exactly a "substitute" for the temple, as many scholars tend to put it. It is an entirely new institution, which without exaggeration may be considered one of the greatest innovations in the history of religions, as it is acknowledged to be by some historians of religions.[6] In contrast to the house of God, where a layman could come only as a guest and linger in the outer court, being denied access to the inner cultic sanctity, which remained the sole prerogative of priests, the synagogue is a democratic institution in its character (as far as the concept "democracy" is applicable in this context). It first appeared sometime during the Second Temple period, and by Hellenistic times it was already a well-established institution.[7] From several indications in the Mishnah we know that there was a synagogue on the Temple Mount itself, in the inner courtyard, while talmudic traditions speak of hundreds of synagogues in Jerusalem before its destruction.[8]

From this point of view, the Second Temple period was one of transition in the history of Judaism, as during that time Judaism

6. See, e.g., C. H. Toy, *Introduction to the History of Religions* (Cambridge: Harvard University, 1913) 546; G. F. Moore, *History of Religions* (New York: Scribner, 1919) 2:62–63; likewise Filson, *Biblical Archaeologist* 7 (1944) 83–84.

7. Since the synagogue became so typical of Jewish communal life, it was the traditional premise that this institution is as old as Judaism itself and was founded by Moses. This premise is to be found in various statements of Midrash and in the writings of Philo (*Vita Mosis*, II: 215–16) and Josephus (*Contra Apionem* 2:17) as well as in the New Testament (Acts 15:21). However, this is a mere projection of an existing institution back onto the past. Historically speaking, we have no evidence for the existence of synagogues before the Hellenistic period (though this does not eliminate the possibility that their first spores could have appeared toward the end of the Persian period). Of those who argue for a high antiquity of the synagogue, mention may here be made of L. Finkelstein, "The Origin of the Synagogue," *Proceedings of the American Academy for Jewish Research* 1 (1928–30) 49–59, whose proposal to trace the origins of this institution in the prophetic movement of the First Temple period is totally untenable. Even the position taken in this respect by S. Zeitlin ("The Origin of the Synagogue," *Proceedings of the American Academy for Jewish Research* 2 [1930–31] 69–81), e.g., who also refers to G. F. Moore, that "the synagogue as a fixed institution was in existence in Babylonia after the destruction of the first temple" (ibid., 73), seems to me highly farfetched.

8. For the synagogue in the Second Temple's inner courtyard, see *m. Yoma* 7:8; *m. Taʿan.* 2:5; *m. Sot.* 7:7–8. For the talmudic traditions, see *b. Ketub.* 105a; *y. Meg.* 3:1 (73d).

reached the stage at which it could practically give up the institution of the house of God altogether. Consequently, when the Second Temple fell, Judaism could absorb the blow without collapsing. The temple was thus turned into an eschatological symbol, to be resurrected only at the end of days, while for the ongoing daily life new frameworks and channels of communal activity were found.

Yet, even though the synagogue is mainly a gathering place for praying, prayer itself, far from being the synagogue's creation, originated in much earlier periods and, like sacrifice, is one of the earliest manifestations of human spirit. Prayer was also prevalent in the temple courts, and it is no mere coincidence that one of the prophets applies the epithet "house of prayer" to the temple (Isa 56:7). In Solomon's prayer on the inauguration of the temple built by him, the temple is also described as a place of prayer, while sacrifices are not even mentioned (1 Kgs 8:22–53). In the temple, however, prayer was considered a gesture of secondary order. There it was a substitute for sacrifice, a kind of "offering of the poor": a visitor to the temple was ideally expected to bring an offering to the Lord, but if he came empty-handed he was at least supposed to utter a prayer, which would be a sort of substitute. Such an understanding of prayer as being secondary to sacrifice finds explicit expression in the Book of Psalms, the collection of Jerusalem Temple prayers. Thus we find a supplicant asking that his prayer "be taken like incense" before the Lord, and his "upraised hands" (that is, the palms raised upward in a customary gesture of prayer), be accepted "like an evening grain-offering" (Ps 141:2). When the psalmist says "accept, O Lord, the free-will offering of my mouth" (Ps 119:108) he actually expects that his words will be as acceptable as a free-will sacrifice. When he declares that "sacrifices to God are a broken spirit" and proclaims that God "will not despise the contrite and crushed of heart" (Ps 51:19), he has no intention of renouncing sacrifices as such but merely indicates the fact that "a broken spirit" is all he can offer and sets forth his hope that this spirit will count for him as if it were a sacrifice.

Thus, within the framework of temple service, as it was carried out in the First Temple of Jerusalem, sacrifice could not usually be done without, while prayer was optional.[9] The decisive fact is that whereas bringing offerings is frequently referred to in the Pentateuch as a categorical obligation, there is no mention of a requirement to

---

9. This is the case despite the fact that such sacrifices as free-will offering, or votive offering, were brought as a matter of individual decision (however, the type of sin- or guilt-offering was considered, under certain conditions, obligatory from the outset).

pray to God.[10] In ancient Israel, then, prayer belonged to the periphery of cult and in fact was not a part of cultic activity. Its place was outside the priestly circle which, within the temple area, held sole responsibility for all cultic matters.

Offerings, Prayer, Prostrations

What, then, did an ordinary Israelite, a member of his community in ancient Israel, do when he wished to worship his God? The highest obligation laid upon him would be to bring an oblation—an offering, either burnt- or peace-offering, or at least a grain-offering. According to biblical concepts, worship is tantamount to sacrificing. A sacrifice could be offered either at a solitary altar (not attached to a temple) or at an open cultic place (where, by the altar, were found some additional cultic objects, such as a pillar, a sacred tree). But it was especially desirable to bring the sacrifice to a house of God. There the man would turn to the priest, lay his hand on the head of the sacrificial animal, and sometimes perform the slaughtering himself; with this his part would be practically over. All the activities involved in the actual execution of the offering on the altar were the concern of the priest, while after burning the fats, all that remained for the sacrificer to do, in case it was a peace-offering, was to consume the meat of the offering in ritual purity and also to honor the priest with his duly allotted portions.

If a person was unable to bring an oblation and had to come to the temple empty-handed, as most of the people probably did, he would at least be required to utter a prayer. Even this matter, however, would be far from simple. In most cases prayers were recited in formulaic fashion and in poetical language. The supplicant would have to acquire a ready-made version, cast in conventional form, after the pattern of psalmodic poetry, many examples of which were eventually assembled in the biblical Psalter. In all likelihood, it would have been considered improper and disrespectful to utter to God, in his Temple, spontaneous words, as they would come to the petitioner's mind on the spur of the moment.[11] If the man did not even say a

10. The Rabbis were able to derive such a commandment from the Pentateuch only indirectly, by explaining the verse in Deut 11:13, " . . . and to serve him with all your heart," as referring to prayer (see Sifre, par. *Eqeb* 41).

11. Prose prayers, which biblical authors occasionally put in the mouths of certain figures, can possibly be explained as a prosaic reporting of content which, under actual conditions, had better been expressed in formulaic language and in the solemn form of poetical style. Reporting the petitioner's main intention in prose sentences is possibly easier for the author and is also not disruptive of the narrative framework. In any case,

prayer he would at least have to prostrate himself before the Lord, a
practice to which the people still adhered at the end of the Second
Temple period, at which time it was customary to pay obeisance in
front of breaches in the railings surrounding the inner Temple precincts, as well as opposite the gates of the inner court and in the
course of the Day of Atonement ceremony.[12] Prostration is a practice
in itself which became habitual in certain religions, but was never
really adopted by the synagogue.[13]

In reality these three gestures, even though they come in descend-
ing order of importance, joined and complemented each other. One
who entered the temple court would prostrate himself upon arrival
and before his departure (cf. 1 Sam 1:3, 19) and he would do the
same even if he intended to offer a sacrifice, which likewise did not
eliminate the possibility of reciting a prayer. The prayer itself was also
accompanied by prostrations (Ps 5:8; 95:6; 99:5, 9, et al.; cf. Isa 44:17;
45:14). Prostration, however, was the absolute minimum expected
from anyone who bothered to come to the house of God. Indeed, it
seems quite probable that many visitors to the temple court contented
themselves with prostration (Jer 7:2; 26:2; Ezek 46:3, 9, et al.), as this
gesture was taken to be a sufficient expression of paying homage.
Thus, one of the prophets promises that those lost and dispersed in
Assyria and Egypt will come "and prostrate themselves before the
Lord in the holy mountain, in Jerusalem" (Isa 27:13). Still another
declares that "on every New Moon and Sabbath day, all mankind will
come to prostrate themselves" before the Lord (Isa 66:23).

Conclusion

In sum, the service of God in the strict sense of the word, that is,
the offering of sacrifices, was supplemented in the temple court by

---

the biblical evidence must be brought in line with the general history of prayer, which
evolved from fixed forms to free prose and from the formulaic to the spontaneous.
Prayer as non-mediated expression is apparently a relatively modern phenomenon and
belongs at the end of the process rather than at the beginning. For the beginnings of
prayer were, of necessity, rooted in the transitional stage from a magical conception of
the world to an apprehension of personal deity; cf. on this matter S. Mowinckel,
Religion and Kultus (Göttingen: Vandenhoeck & Ruprecht, 1953) 13–30. Indeed, from
the historical point of view, in Mowinckel's system, set "cultic" prayer is given precedence over personal free prayer (ibid., 115–21) and in this respect he really seems to be
on the right side.

12. See *m. Mid.* 2:3, 6; *m. Šeqal.* 6:1, 3. For the prostrations on the Day of
Atonement, *m. Yoma* 6:2; *m. ʾAbot* 5:5.

13. *Masgid*, the Arabic term for mosque, means literally 'place of prostration'. In
fact, the mosque is a kind of "house of prostration," inasmuch as Muslim prayer is

prayer and prostrations. The three acts complemented each other, serving as constituents of the broader temple complex, in which the idea of the house of God manifested itself. In the period of the Second Temple, however, prayer as an act of worship was also implanted in a distinct institutional framework in the form of a synagogue, which was an entirely new innovation. In the course of time this institution enabled Judaism to do without the temple altogether. In fact, the emergence of the new institution during the Second Temple period was only one of the pointers of the fact that in that temple certain basic features of the house of God were dimmed (not the least of these is the very architectural layout of the Second Temple in its Herodian stage, as reflected in the Mishnah Middot).

---

mainly based on kneeling and bowing down, and in this respect the mosque possesses a special quality which is not to be found in the synagogue.

The Meaning and Function of
the Temple in Classical Greece

WALTER BURKERT

GREEK CIVILIZATION has been called a "temple culture,"[1] and this characterization will sound convincing to everyone who has come to Greece, Paestum, or Sicily. It is the temples that occupy the place of pride in ancient Greek cities, as in the modern tourist's routes. It is in the temples that Greek art and architecture reached their peak, and classicistic style found its permanent model. By contrast, one could speak of a "palace culture" in Minoan Crete or in Europe of the 17th and 18th centuries; late antiquity became an amphitheater- and thermae-culture; ours would probably be characterized as a highway culture. Yet there are evident practical reasons for highways, as there are for public baths.

It is less clear why man needs religion. But the very paradox of the Greek temple is that it seems to be most contingent where it most properly belongs, in Greek religion. Why did the Greeks, in the poor conditions of what would be a third-world economy today, concentrate on elaborating the superfluous, that which at first and second glance and on their own reflection they did not really need?

There are difficulties, though, not only with the answer but with the question itself. It is the problem of generalization both in a synchronic and a diachronic perspective. The genesis of the Greek temple is quite well documented by now; it is a complicated history with many strands.[2] To give just a few indications: no tradition of temple building was to survive the catastrophe that befell the Greek world about 1200 B.C. Greek language persisted, including a set of gods' names and cult terms, a few sanctuaries remained in permanent use, but there is no continuity in architecture and hardly any in figurative art from the Bronze Age to the Geometric period. A single sacred

1. I owe this designation to Karl Schefold. He, however, disclaims having coined the term.
2. See esp. Drerup 1969; Kalpaxis 1976; Coldstream 1985; and Mazarakis-Ainian 1985.

structure of late Mycenaean times (12th century B.C.) was preserved at Cyprus, the "temple" of Wanassa-Aphrodite of Paphos, but it was totally different from a normal Greek temple.[3]

From about 800 B.C. onward "temples," single independent buildings devoted to the cult of a definite god or goddess, can be identified in quite diverse forms of architecture: there are horseshoe forms and rectangular forms, comparatively short or very long ones. It seems that practically all forms of houses were tried until the old megaron type prevailed, the oblong rectangular form with entrance from the small side—normally from the east—and often provided with a front hall. The sacred measure of 100 feet, *hekatompedon*, is found at the first Heraion of Samos. The *peristasis* of wooden columns surprisingly appears at Lefkandi, Euboea (in the 10th century B.C.), with a spectacular yet short-lived building where a prince and his wife were buried; whether it should be called a *heroon* is controversial; at any rate, it was not a temple of the normal kind.[4] Later a wooden *peristasis* was added to the Samian temple. It was a practical as well as aesthetic device, protecting mudbrick walls by the extension of the roof.

The familiar form of the Greek temple developed during the 7th century B.C., with the use of carefully worked stone blocks and the invention of roof tiles that determined the form of the pediment. Egyptian impressions provided an incentive for stone colonnades.[5] The "Dorian" and the "Ionian" order, with strict rules for the entablature, are established by the 6th century B.C., with little development or change for the centuries to come. It is this standard form which we have in mind, as did Vitruvius, when speaking of "the Greek temple." It was to dominate Mediterranean architecture for nearly 1,000 years. Yet meanings and functions are easier to see in the earlier tentative and variable forms, whereas the persistence of style in later periods is apt to hide basic changes that must have occurred in such a long and eventful history.

3. Preliminary reports by F. G. Maier in *Archäologischer Anzeiger* (1975) 436–46; (1977) 257–85; (1978) 309–16; (1980) 498–511; idem, "Das Heiligtum der Aphrodite in Paphos," *Neue Forschungen in griechischen Heiligtümern* (ed. Ulf Jantzen; Tübingen: Wasmuth, 1977) 219–38; "Alt-Paphos auf Cypern," *6. Trierer Winckelmannsprogramm* (Mainz, 1984) 12–15.

4. On the building of Lefkandi, see *Archaeological Reports* (1981/82) 15–17; (1982/83) 12–15; M. R. Popham et al., "The Hero of Lefkandi," *Antiquity* 51 (1982) 169–71; P. Blome, "Lefkandi und Homer," *Würzburger Jahrbücher* 10 (1984) 9–22; Mazarakis-Ainian 1985: 6–9.

5. See G. Hölbl, "Aegyptischer Einfluss in der griechischen Architektur," *Oester-reichische Jahreshefte* 55 (1984) 1–18. On the development of *peristasis*, see Mallwitz 1981 and Martini 1986; on its practical function, Coldstream 1985: 71. Mallwitz (624–33) has lowered the date of the first Samian temple by about one century to the beginning of the 7th century B.C.

But even if we concentrate on the three centuries from about 600 to 300 B.C., the period within which most of the important Greek temples were built, there is enormous diversity. Leaving aside eccentricities such as the temple of Didyma, which is really an open-air spring sanctuary within a colonnade, or the problem of the Segesta temple, which lacks a cella altogether,[6] we have the Parthenon of Athens, a unique masterpiece of architecture and plastic art; or the Apollo temple of Delphi, light-flooded columns in a magnificent landscape; or the temple of Zeus in Olympia, with its prostrate yet superhuman column drums; or the temple of Hera at Samos, one of the oldest among the major temple sites. Yet each of these four exemplars is an exception in one aspect or another. The Parthenon was a temple with very little cult, if any, and was not connected with any of the old great festivals of the city or the traditional priesthoods of Athens. Olympia, by contrast, had had the cult without a temple for centuries (the temple and statue of Zeus were a comparatively late addition to the games and to the altar). The Samos shrine had a movable statue to be brought out during a festival and back in again afterward; originally it had been just a plank.[7] The Delphic temple never had a cult statue but had peculiar installations for the oracle that was the god's epiphany. In a similar way, most generalizations will need qualification in every particular case, and the peculiarities may even appear to be more interesting than the common and comparatively banal features.

In spite of this, some basic phenomena about *the* Greek temple—an ideal type perhaps that does not exist as such but is still recognizable with slight variations in multiple exemplars—will be described. The focus will be first on the idea of a temple as expressed in language, literature, and architecture, then on the use made of temples in the actual cult, and finally on its relationships to the political and social system to which it belongs.

The Idea of a Temple

A temple is no doubt considered the "house" of a god. This is evidently equivalent to the Near Eastern usage, Sumerian *é-*, Akkadian *bit-*, etc., meaning both 'house' and 'temple'. The Greek term is *nāos*, Ionian *nēos*, Attic *neōs*, related to *naiein*, 'to dwell'. The only anomaly, contrasting with the eastern parallel, is that the substantive *nāos* exclusively refers to temples and never to a private building, whereas

---

6. For Didyma, see Gruben 1984: 359–75; for Segesta, Gruben 1984: 315–17; D. Mertens, *Der Tempel von Segesta* (Mainz: Zabern, 1984).

7. See H. Walter, *Das Heraion von Samos* (Munchen: Piper, 1976); Burkert 1985: 134f.; on the date of the first temple, see n. 5; Mazarakis-Ainian 1985: 21.

the verb is commonly used with all kinds of subjects. This is established already in the Homeric language. The case of Linear B is unclear: '*woikos* of the Lady (*Potnia*)' occurs at Thebes, but whether *woikos*, which means 'house' in later Greek, designates a temple, a precinct, or a district is a problem of its own.[8] Later it remains possible to use all the common words for 'house' to refer to a temple—(*w*)*oikos, domos, doma*—besides the term *nāos*, which seems to mark the separation of immortals from mortals. Another way to designate a sanctuary, in Mycenaean as in later Greek, is to use an adjective derived from the god's name: *Posidaïon, Apollonion, Heraion*; this usage deprives us of a special term for 'temple'.

The divinity is presumed to reside in his or her temple. The *Hymn to Demeter* has Zeus sitting in his temple to receive splendid offerings (lines 28f.) and Demeter retreating to her temple to avoid the company of other gods (lines 300ff.). Vase paintings show the god enthroned between columns, i.e., within a temple.[9] Of course the gods are free to move, but they like to come back to their own houses: thus Aphrodite goes to Paphos (*Od.* 8,363); Athena to Athens to the 'house of Erechtheus' which she is sharing (*Od.* 7,81); Apollo carries Aineias off to his temple at Troy where his mother and his sister, Leto and Artemis, are equally present to take care of him (*Il.* 5,446f.). But Homer and the other poets also imagine the gods living together in pleasant company in the 'housings of Olympus', be this a mountain or simply Heaven. The latter designations would exclude their permanent presence in any of their 'houses' on earth; anyhow it is known that the 'much-venerated' gods have many dwellings in various places. In poetic imagination the gods do a good deal of rapid traveling, and their momentary absence adds a convenient narrative motif to many tales. In ritual hymns, the tradition of which seems to go back to Indo-European heritage, the gods are invoked to leave their heavenly abode, to mount their chariot, and to come to the

8. Tablet TH Of 36: T. G. Spyropoulos and J. Chadwick, *The Thebes Tablets* (Salamanca: University of Salamanca, 1975), 2:102; cf. pp. 88f. on the interpretation of the text, and a possible opposition between *wôikos*, 'house of a god', and *do*, 'house of a man'. The only possible trace of the word *naos* in Mycenaean Greek is the mentioning of *khalkos nawijos* in the tablet from Pylos PY Jn 829, but the meaning is quite uncertain: 'bronze from the temple'? 'bronze from houses'? 'bronze from/for the ships'? See A. Leukart "Autour de *ka-ko na-wi-jo*: quelques critères," in *Colloquium Mycenaeum, Actes du VIe Colloque international sur les textes mycéniens et égéens* (Neuchâtel: University of Neuchâtel, 1979) 183–87.

9. See, e.g., Apollo at Delphi on the volute crater at the Kleophon-painter from Spina: N. Alfieri and P. E. Arias, *Spina* (Munich: Hirmer, 1958) pls. 85, 87; an unknown god ('Sabazios') in his temple, ibid., pls. 74f.; Nossis, *Anthologia Palatina* 6.265,2, addressing Hera Lakinia: "you come from heaven and survey your fragrant sanctuary."

place of sacrifice: it is there that they receive their worshipers, who bring offerings and all kinds of honors. In some cases there are seasonal festivals to celebrate the advent of a god, e.g., the festival of Apollo at Delphi.[10] Normally it is presumed that the ritual will attract the god even apart from a predetermined schedule.

The temple is the house of the god: in concrete terms, this means that the temple is a permanent building to house the statue of the respective divinity.[11] Temple building thus goes together with the development of plastic art. The Paphos temple did not contain an anthropomorphic image but a sacred stone, and the temple at Samos originally held a plank, but during the 8th and 7th centuries B.C. plastic art made spectacular progress. It seems that most of the 'sacred' cult images from this period were in fact wooden carvings. The older ones were smaller than life size, but Apollon at Delos got a colossal gilded statue already in archaic times. Classical art developed the big chryselephantine images to match the proportions of the temple or even to surpass them: if Zeus at Olympia were to rise from his seat, he would unroof the temple, Strabo wrote (8, p. 353).

The normal temple had one cult image set up in the inner room, generally called the *cella*—in Greek this is the *nāos* proper—frontally facing the entrance. The single cult image is a marked contrast to Minoan and Mycenaean practice, where we find multiple statuettes, mostly small figurines, set up on a bench together with other paraphernalia.[12] An intermediate case is presented by the temple of Dreros, Crete, from the 8th century B.C.: it had a hearth, a deposit of goat horns, and a bench at the side on which there were bronze statues of Apollo, Leto, and Artemis, manufactured in *sphyrelaton* technique. They may possibly be called the earliest and only surviving cult statues.[13]

Normally the cult images, made of wood, had no chance of being preserved through the ages. The usual term for the statue was just

---

10. Burkert 1985: 146f.; idem, *Homo Necans: The Anthropology of Ancient Greek Sacrificial Ritual and Myth* (Berkeley: University of California, 1983) 123–30.

11. See the comprehensive account of Funke 1981; Burkert 1985: 88–92; I. B. Romano, "Early Cult Images" (Diss. Univ. of Pennsylvania, 1980); H. Jung, *Thronende und sitzende Götter: Zum griechischen Götterbild und Menschenideal in geometrischer und fr21harchaischer Zeit* (Bonn: Habelt, 1982); B. Gladigow, "Zur Konkurrenz von Bild und Namen im Aufbau theistischer Systeme," *Wort und Bild* (ed. H. Brunner, R. Kannicht, and K. Schwager; Munich: Fink, 1977) 103–22.

12. See R. Hägg and N. Marinatos, ed., *Sanctuaries and Cults in the Aegean Bronze Age* (Stockholm: Svenska Institutet; Athen, 1981); B. Rutkowski, *The Cult Places of the Aegean* (New Haven: Yale University, 1986).

13. S. Marinatos, "Le temple géométrique de Dréros," *Bulletin de Correspondence Hellénique* 60 (1936) 214–56; J. Boardman, *The Cretan Collection in Oxford*

xoanon, 'wood carving'; poets use the term *bretas,* a word without etymology; more telling is the official designation as *hedos,* 'what is made to sit': the cult statue is made to 'settle' in a way that does not permit it to be moved again. The respective ritual is expressed by the verb *hidryein,* derived from the same root 'to sit'. We do not know all the details of *hidrysis*; food set up in pots and eaten ceremoniously played a role.[14] If in another place a temple of the same god was to be erected or rededicated, certain objects, called *aphidrymata,* would be taken from the original sanctuary to be placed in the new abode. Foundation offerings such as are common in the East occur in archaic Greek temple building too, e.g., at Delos and at Ephesus.[15]

The advent of temple building and cult statues of the type indicated was a comparatively late phenomenon in Greek civilization. It was never forgotten that the major gods of Indo-European and Mycenaean tradition, Zeus and Poseidon, did not need a temple, and that the images were man-made. Soon philosophy stepped in to criticize anthropomorphism and to idealize a past when men experienced the divine in groves and celestial phenomena without man-made appurtenances.[16] Certain images were said to have 'fallen from heaven' and were credited with a sort of magical power, but such a treasure was hidden from the public and was not a normal cult statue; foremost of all was the Trojan *Palladion,* a portable statuette of armed Athena that was claimed to be in the possession of Athens, of Argos, and of Rome.[17] By the time of St. Paul the image of Ephesian Artemis too was described as 'fallen from heaven' (Acts 19:35).

It is natural that popular superstition would cling to the images, that signs such as change of color or 'sweating' and 'weeping' should be attentively observed and interpreted as important omens. But usually one also remembered the artist who had done the carving, or even invented mythical craftsmen for the purpose. Heraclitus said that praying to statues was like talking to houses (B 5). Even less sophisticated worshipers did not simply identify statue and god. Vase

---

(Oxford: Clarendon, 1961) 137; I. Beyer, *Die Tempel von Dreros und Prinias A und die Chronologie der kretischen Kunst des 8. und 7. Jh. v. Chr.* (Freiburg: Oberkirch, 1976).

14. See G. Hock, *Griechische Weihegebräuche* (Würzburg: Sturz, 1905).

15. See W. Burkert, "Die orientalisierende Epoche in der griechischen Religion und Literatur," *Sitzungsberichte der Heidelberger Akademie der Wissenschaften* 1 (1984) 55–57; U. Sinn, "Der sog. Tempel D im Heraion von Samos II: Ein archäologischer Befund aus der nachpolykratischen Zeit. Mit einem Exkurs zum griechischen Bauopfer," *Mitteilungen des deutschen archäologischen Instituts, Athenische Abteilung* 100 (1985) 129–58, esp. 134–40, 142f.

16. See Funke 1981: 745–56; Gladigow, "Zur Konkurrenz" (above, n. 11), with older literature.

17. See Burkert 1977: 140, and n. 11 above.

paintings make a clear distinction and sometimes represent both statue and god side by side.[18] The same occurs on stage in Aeschylus' *Eumenides*: "I am coming to your image, O Goddess," Orestes says to Athena in Athens (242). There are offering tables (*trapezai*) in the temples to display food offered to the gods, to be consumed by the priests in due course. But we know nothing about elaborate ceremonies to bring the statues to life, to feed them, to awaken them in the morning, and put them to bed at night, as is done in adjacent civilizations. Gods are provided with garments, it is true; these are sometimes brought in public procession at the festivals and 'laid on the knees' of the divinity (*Il.* 6,92), along with all kinds of private textile dedications. In a way this may look back to aboriginal customs of hanging animal hides, fillets, and garments from a sacred tree.[19]

Since a favorite offering to a god was an image of this very god, statuettes and statues would multiply within a sanctuary or even within a single temple. Nor would a god reject offerings of images of other gods from his family. These additional images usually were votive offerings, *anathemata*. In fact, most of the famous archaic, classical, or Hellenistic statues preserved either in the original or in later copies belong to this category. But there is not even sharp separation between cult image and *anathema*. The ritual of *hidrysis* apparently did not leave distinctive marks, and it even could be undone by 'pleasing' rituals, *aresteria*, to win the god's consent for a change. Thus the image of Hera from Tiryns, counted among the most ancient and venerable divine statues of Greece, was moved to the Argive Heraion where Pausanias still saw it (2,17,5), a curiosity rather than a cult-object.

If we try to understand the design of a Greek temple as a 'house of the god', it is advisable to refrain from delving into elaborate worlds of symbolism. The Greek temple could hardly be called the tomb of the god or the goddess's bridal chamber. It is not normally considered the center of the universe or the axis of heaven and earth, *pace* Mircea Eliade's phenomenology of the sacred.[20] Delphi, called

18. Common in representations of Ajax, Cassandra, and the Trojan Palladion: *Lexicon Iconographicum Mythologiae Classicae* (Zürich: Artemis, 1981), vol. 1, s.v. Aias II nos. 54–58; Apollo-statue and Apollo as god: Lucanian bell-crater of the Pisticci painter, *Antike Kunstwerke aus der Sammlung Ludwig* (ed. E. Berger and R. Lullies; Basel: Archäologischer Verlag Basel, 1979) 183 no. 70.

19. The evidence is collected in the old study of C. Boetticher, *Der Baumkultus der Hellenen* (Berlin: Weidmann, 1856) 39–45; see, e.g., *Anthologia Palatina*, 6,35; 57; cf. also K. Meuli, *Gesammelte Schriften* (Basel: Schwabe, 1975), 2:1083–1118.

20. M. Eliade, *The Myth of the Eternal Return* (New York: Pantheon, 1954; French original, *Le mythe de l'éternel retour* [Paris: Gallimard, 1949]); see also R. Bloch

'navel of the earth', is a singular case. For the rest there is no Greek designation comparable to that of the temple tower of Babylon, *E-temen-an-ki* 'House of the foundation of Heaven and Earth'.

Greek temples tend to come in groups—splendid examples survive in Paestum, Selinus, or Agrigento. The rectangular structure is designed to "square" with other departments of reality, in contrast to the symbolism of center and widening circles. Nor is it of much avail to look for special symbolic significance in the details of fluted columns, capitals, metopes, triglyphs, and pediments. The architectural design used for temples was also used for other buildings such as halls, propylaia, and treasuries. It is difficult to say anything in general about the meaning of iconography in temple ornamentation, be it friezes, pediments, or acroteria. General Greek mythology and local traditions, forceful imagery and purely formal conventions are seen to interact in various ways. Sometimes the idea of liminality can be detected, expressed by the foreign or composite monsters, the centaurs, the gorgon, and the animals of prey. At the same time, this is a representation of power. There is a strange predilection for scenes of violence and death in archaic and classical art. This can be seen as reflecting the practice of animal sacrifice and the contrasting exemption from death possessed by the gods. But this is not to be pursued further in this context.

Let us rather start from a characteristic detail that sets the temple apart from a normal 'house': the huge door in the *nāos*, turned towards the rising sun, normally the only source of light for the interior.[21] There is *prosodos* 'access' from the outside to the divinity dwelling inside, who is represented by the statue—"holiest *prósodoi* of the gods," in the words of Aristophanes, are constitutive of Athenian piety

---

et al., *Le symbolisme cosmique des monuments religieux* (Rome: Instituto italiano per il Medio ed Estremo Oriento, 1957). For an infelicitous attempt at analyzing the symbolism of the Greek temple, see H. G. Evers, "Der griechische Tempel," *Das Werk des Künstlers (Hubert Schrade FS*; ed. Hans Fegers; Stuttgart: Kohlhammer, 1960) 1–35. The most detailed studies of the 'navel' (*omphalos*) complex are those of W. H. Roscher, "Omphalos," *Abhandlungen der sächsischen Gesellschaft der Wissenschaften* 29.9 (Leipzig, 1913); "Neue Omphalosstudien," ibid., 31.1 (1915); "Der Omphalosgedanke bei verschiedenen Völkern, besonders den semitischen," *Berichte der sächsischen Gesellschaft der Wissenschaften* 70.2 (Leipzig, 1918). See also H. V. Herrmann, *Omphalos* (Münster: Aschendorff, 1953).

21. Of course this is not exclusively Greek; see, e.g., the model of a Moabite temple in *Vom Euphrat zum Nil: Kunst aus dem alten Ägypten und Vorderasien* (Gesellschaft der Freunde eines Schweizerischen Orient-Museums, Egg/Zürich, 1985) no. 50, and the advice to placate a god by 'seeking his door', W. G. Lambert and A. R. Millard, *Atraḫasis: The Babylonian Story of the Flood* (Oxford: Oxford University, 1969) 68f. (I:380).

(*Clouds* 306f.). Worship means to 'come', to 'turn to' the gods (*hiketeia*, *prostropé*). Access to the divine is not free and simple, but regulated through steps and boundaries; it can be barred and reopened again. This is represented by the figure of the priestess with the big key, the *kleidouchos*, a constant attribute of temple iconography. A temple, though "a unique kind of sculptural image in the landscape" (Scully 1979: 46), does not stand as an isolated block but is surrounded by its premises, the *temenos*. The limits of the *temenos* are marked by stones, *horoi*, or by a wall surrounding the whole place. There is a gate for access, and it is here that water basins, *perirrhanteria*, are placed for the purification of those who wish to enter, for only the pure should pass the boundary. Inside, certain prohibitions are to be observed, especially not to make love, not to give birth, not to let one die within the precinct.

The temple itself is raised above the ground by a basis which forms three huge steps—steps for gods, as they have been called. Then there are the columns flanking the entrance hall, or in the more elaborate examples, the peristyle surrounding the whole of the building. The columns are the most characteristic feature of Greek architecture. For the Greeks they would primarily mean dignity, *semnotes*, and harmony, *rhythmos*; but what columns in fact do is to provide permeable boundaries: you are invited, even attracted to pass through the interstice, but there is an unmistakable distinction between outside and inside, especially as the columns come alive in Greek sunlight. Then there is the huge open door to the cella which is raised by one more step, and from the dusk there emerges the image, facing the visitor as he comes near. The door remains open; the world of sunshine and colors outside will not be forgotten; the boundaries remain permeable from either side. It is in this way that the temple provides access and communication with the divine, through grades to be heeded with care: you may go in, but be conscious of what you are doing. "People who enter a temple and see the images of the gods from near get a different mind" was a saying attributed to Pythagoras (Sen. *ep.* 94,42).

The degrees of sanctity—*temenos*, *nāos*, *hedos*—also play their role in the practice of asylum: to touch the image is the safest place.[22] Some temples had an additional inner room behind the cult image which was not generally accessible, hence called *adyton*, 'not to slip

22. Pictures show Cassandra clinging to the image of Athena, *Lexicon Iconographicum* (above, n. 18) s.v. Aias II nos. 44, 54–90. The 'Kylonians' at Athens bound a cord to the image, Plut. *Solon* 12, 1f., cf. Hdt. 5,71 (Thuc. 1,126,10 has "the altar"). Pausanias flees not to the temple but to some accessory building within the *temenos*, Thuc. 1,134,1.

in'. Access was limited to certain priests, temple servants, or visitors of special status.[23] In Delphi the recess within the temple where the Pythia gave oracles was also called *adyton*. For Plotinus, in the perspective of Neoplatonism, the *adyton* 'beyond the image' gains a new dimension of the absolute Beyond (6,9,11,17), of the spiritual surpassing visible reality. There is no evidence for such ideas in earlier cult practice and there is no 'Holiest of Holies' as in Jerusalem. This additional dimension of the secret and mysterious is effective just because it is not justified by explicit theology. An *adyton* may also simply have served as a storeroom.

The Use of Temples in Cult

Absolutely necessary to a temple, by contrast, is an altar within a sanctuary. Altar, temple, and image—these are the three characteristics of a sacred precinct and hence of religious practice.[24] There is a special dialectic between altar and temple that calls the status of the latter into question.

The main acts of cult within a sanctuary may also be divided into three categories: prayer (*euchai*), sacrifice (*thysiai*), and the setting up of votives (*anathemata*). Yet—and this brings us back to the paradox mentioned in the beginning—the temple is not really needed for any of them.

Aboriginal signs of a sanctuary are the tree, the spring, and the rock. Sacred action *per se* for the Greeks is animal sacrifice together with the ensuing feast. Its center is the open-air altar on which fire is burning: bones, inedibles, and some chosen pieces are burnt for the gods, the smoke and scent go to heaven, and the rest is for the banquet. Through encounter with death, the community of men is enacted in a strange interplay of togetherness with and separation from the gods. The worshipers stand "around the altar," as the texts say, in reality, as topography indicates, often in a semicircle between the temple and the altar.[25] The altar is commonly placed opposite the temple entrance, as is true also in West-Semitic sanctuaries. Facing the altar, the worshipers thus had the temple at their back. This is the arrangement for the main prayer, pronounced by the priest or the

23. Mentioned already in the *Iliad* 5,448; 512; P. Stengel, *Die griechischen Kultusaltertümer* (3d ed.; Munich: Beck, 1920) 25f.; S. K. Thalmann, "The 'Adyton' in the Greek Temples of South Italy and Sicily" (Diss.; University of California, Berkeley, 1978); M. B. Hollinghead, "Against Iphigeneia's Adyton in Three Mainland Temples," *American Journal of Archaeology* 89 (1985) 419–40; Delphi: Paus. 10,24,4.

24. Cf. Hdt. 1,131; 2,4,2; 4,59; 4,108,2; Plat. *leg.* 738c.

25. See Bergquist 1967: 112–14; on sacrifice in general, see Burkert 1985: 55–59, and *Homo Necans* (above, n. 10) *pass.*

lord of sacrifice immediately before the slaughter. Many festivals take place in the morning; this makes people turn their faces, while praying and sacrificing, towards the rising sun, the rays of which would reach the image through the temple door at the same time. Thus the temple, built as a façade, provides a magnificent background for the ritual, but no more.

It is true that older structures, from the 8th and 7th centuries B.C., have a hearth within the rectangular building. Burning of offerings as well as the preparation of meals and common feasting could go on there. This has given rise to controversy as to whether or not a building of this kind should be considered a special form of temple, the "archaic *Herdhaus* temple," or rather a banqueting hall, *hestiatorion*, and what should make the decisive difference.[26] This problem need not be solved here. In the case of Dreros (n. 13 above) the term "temple" seems to be justified by the horn deposit and by the images on the side bench. The temple of Delphi always had a sacred *hestia*, an ever-burning hearth inside, but no cult statue. But in normal Greek custom the *nāos* would have been cleared of these installations and reserved for the abode of the god.

Special banqueting halls called *leschai* were added in the major sanctuaries; this word possibly is connected with Hebrew *liškā*, which designates a similar building.[27] In this way the god's dwelling place and the feast of the mortals remain connected but neatly separated. No man would dwell within the *nāos* unless he was a stupid *barbaros*; even to reside in the back hall was *hybris* characteristic of a Hellenistic king.[28] Piety means to respect demarcations: "Know thyself," you are not a god.

Setting up permanent tokens of worship in a sanctuary is a very old practice too. With the rise of craftsmanship and wealth at the close of the Dark Ages this practice underwent an unprecedented expansion. All sorts of prestige objects were created to be accumulated in the sacred areas: vessels, weapons, garments, statuettes, costly bronze tripods, or even bricks of gold.[29] It was the riches of these

26. See Drerup 1969: 123-28, for the type of "Herdhaus-Tempel" and *contra* Bergquist, *Herakles on Thasos* (Uppsala: University of Uppsala, 1973) 61f.; Martini 1986.

27. This was already pointed out by W. R. Smith, *Lectures on the Religion of the Semites* (2d ed.; London: Black, 1894) 254 n. 6.

28. Artayktes the Persian had sexual intercourse in the Adyton of Protesilaos (Hdt. 9,116); Demetrios Poliorketes dwelt in the Parthenon's *opisthodomos* (Plut. *Demetr.* 23f.). Even Agesilaos dwelt in sanctuaries, though conducting himself properly (Xenoph. *Ages.* 5,7).

29. See Burkert 1985: 92-95; an unsurpassed older study is W. H. D. Rouse, *Greek Votive Offerings* (Cambridge: Cambridge University, 1902). *Anathemata* "within" the

anathemata that chiefly constituted the splendor of a sanctuary. Some
of these would be placed within the temple itself, even within the
cella. Dedicants naturally wished their gifts to be close to the attention
of the god. Shields from the booty of wars were hung on the temple
walls. But it was neither possible nor necessary that all these objects
should be inside the temple. Bigger votives remained in the open air
and special halls were constructed to protect the ordinary samples. At
Olympia and Delphi the major communities built their own 'treasuries'
(*thesauroi*) in the form of minor temples to hold their offerings per-
manently. 'Precinct governors' (*tamiai*) or sacristans with common
sense had to ensure that some order would prevail amidst the multi-
tude of votives that kept accruing. From time to time heaps of them
would simply be buried in the ground (within the sacred enclosure,
to be sure) to keep the god's property unimpaired.

Sacrifice and other offerings always are accompanied by prayer.
In the course of animal sacrifice there is a loud and stately prayer
immediately before the slaughter at the altar: hands are raised to
heaven, as the Homeric formulas have it. Temple and cult statue
remain in the back. One writer suggests that the sacrificial animal was
"led to the image" before the ritual slaughter (Dion *or*. 31,10), but this
cannot have been the rule for the normal flocks of victims. There is no
doubt, nevertheless, that the temple was entered regularly for prayer
in view of the cult statue. The pious would greet the statue with a
gesture of kissing, either falling down on their knees or trying to touch
the statue, kiss it directly.[30] These forms of worship could be done by
officials, by priests and political leaders, even by commoners in pro-
cessions in the course of a festival, but above all by private individuals
who wished to get close to the god. Oaths, important acts for all
business transactions, could be taken in view of the image (Paus.
5,24,9). The Trojan women wished to deposit the garment for Athena
directly on the knees of the image (*Il*. 6,92; 303), and Cassandra is
represented as clinging to the image of Athena when she is raped by
Ajax the Locrian.[31] The gesture of extending one's hands towards the
statue as a sign of urgent entreaty is quite common. There was no

---

temple are mentioned by Homer *Od*. 12,346f. Tripod cauldrons have their counterpart
in Solomon's temple (1 Kgs 7:27–39).

30. For the kinds of worship performed in temples, see Corbett 1970; for appropriate gestures: G. Neumann, *Gesten und Gebärden in der griechischen Kunst* (Berlin:
de Gruyter, 1965) 77–85; A. Delatte, "Le baiser, l'agenouillement et le prosternement de
l'adoration chez les grecs," *Bulletin de la classe des lettres de l'Académie Royale de
Belgique* 37 (1951) 423–50; F. T. van Straten, "Did the Greeks Kneel Before Their
Gods," *Bulletin Antieke Beschaving* 49 (1974) 159–89.

31. See n. 22.

dogma to decide between the heavenly abode of a god and his or her presence in a temple, and worshipers could well try both turning to the sky and to the image in ritual.

Seen from afar, the temple as a whole would be the most visible part of a sanctuary or even of a city, indicating the place to turn to for those who needed help. In the midst of the battle of Plataea, Pausanias the commander "raised his eyes towards the Hera sanctuary" and called the goddess to intervene, and success immediately ensued (Hdt. 9,61,3). It was good to have a stately temple building to provide orientation when in chaos and distress.

This is not to overlook the fact that it was the blending of the aesthetic-artistic element with the religious that made the deepest impression on receptive minds. The anxious concern to make use of the gods on various occasions of need seems to give way time and again to admiring views from a distance. There is not just fear and awe in Greek religion but 'wonder', *thauma*, related to *thea*, the full, admiring look. It was especially with the Pheidias statue of Zeus at Olympia that admiration of art was said to turn into religious experience. "I think that a man, full of weariness in his soul, who has suffered from many misfortunes and pains and cannot even find pleasant sleep, if he stood suddenly in front of this image, would forget all the awful and grievous things to be experienced in human life," an orator wrote (Dion *or.* 12,51). And the Roman general Aemilius Paulus, coming to Olympia in 167 B.C. and entering the temple, was struck by awe beyond all expectation; he ordered sacrifice to be performed as if he were on the Capitolium of Rome (Polyb. 20,10,6; Liv. 45,28). The monument of art had touched the fringe of revelation.

Temples and Polis System

If timeless fascination is felt to emanate from Greek temples, it is still necessary to integrate the phenomenon into the social and symbolic system of its proper time and place. It is evident that the Greek temple is intimately connected with the Greek *polis* structure. Both evolve together and remain mutually interdependent.[32] Temples are normally built by the decree and under the supervision of the city-state. The building program of the acropolis which resulted in the

---

32. See Snodgrass 1977; Polignac 1984; W. Burkert, "Anfänge der Polisreligion," *Comité International des sciences historiques, XVIᵉ Congrès International des sciences historiques, Rapports I* (Stuttgart: Comité International des sciences historiques, 1985), 1:295-97.

Parthenon, the propylaia, and the Erechtheion at Athens is only the best-known example. If tyrants were active in temple building, this was to identify themselves with the city-state. The case seems to be more complicated with Panhellenic sanctuaries such as Delos, Delphi, or Olympia, but there too it was "political" organizations that were in charge of the administration, the funds, and the buildings; there was no theocracy under the guidance of a high priest.

For if, in theory, the god is the owner of his *temenos* and his "house," it is the state that controls the real estate, the buildings, and the treasures. There are various boards of supervisors, 'precinct governors' (*tamiai, epimeletai*)[33] who are responsible to the *demos* especially for the finances of which they have to render account every year; they are elected like other officials. Even the priests are appointed by the organs of the city-state; "the Trojans" had made Theano priestess of Athena, the *Iliad* says (6,300). Priesthoods can also be sold for the benefit of the fiscus. As the temples are the most solid structures of the city, they are used to house the state treasure, behind thick stone walls and heavy and well-locked doors, since religious awe would not suffice to protect money. Thus the opisthodome of the Parthenon served to hold Athena's property and the assets of Athens. The distinction between them could easily be lost. Of course one should not deprive the god of his or her property, but it was possible to make loans, and in times of distress some *anathemata* could be melted down; and yet the denunciation of *hierosylia*, temple-robbery, was close at hand. In happier times temple and city would thrive together.

Temples, archaeologically identifiable as free-standing buildings not devoted to profane use, become prominent with the rise of the *polis* after the 8th century B.C. In some cases it has been found that the temples came as an afterthought: in Smyrna the city walls are older than the first temple; in Megara Hyblaia, Sicily, the temples appear about one century after the foundation of the city. In Eretria, on the other hand, another city newly established in the 8th century B.C., the sanctuary of Apollo is present from the beginning, even if the first structures were quite unlike the later temple of normal type.[34] Homer

33. See Stengel (above, n. 23) 48–53; B. Jordan, *Servants of the Gods* (Göttingen: Vandenhoeck & Ruprecht, 1979); K. Clinton, *The Sacred Officials of the Eleusinian Mysteries* (Philadelphia: American Philosophical Society, 1974); Burkert 1985: 95–98. For building costs, see Burford 1965.

34. E. Akurgal, *Alt-Smyrna I: Wohnschichten und Athena-Tempel* (Ankara: Türk Tarıh, 1983); G. Vallet, F. Villard, and P. Auberson, *Mégara Hyblaea I: Le Quartier de l'agora archaïque* (Rome: École Française de Rome, 1976) 418–21; P. Auberson, *Temple d'Apollon Daphnéphoros* (Bern: Francke, 1968); cf. *Antike Kunst* 17 (1974) 60–68.

is explicit about an ideal city: when Nausithoos founded the town of
the Phaeacians in the form of a "modern" colonial settlement, he
"erected a wall for the town, he built the houses, he made the temples
of the gods, and he divided up the arable land" (*Od.* 6,9f.). These
then are the constitutive acts for the formation of a *polis* and they
include the temples from the start. The poet of the Iliad presumes
that Troy, too, had its temples: at least one for Athena, the city
goddess, at the acropolis (6,88)—as in reality Athena was the city
goddess of Aeolian Ilion—and one for Apollo (5,446).

The example of the Phaeacians is a reminder of the fact that the
formation of the Greek *polis* nearly coincides with the colonization
period. Two factors that were operative in the colonization process
had their impact on the installation of temples: the "division of the
land," and the prominence of military organization. "To divide up the
land," as Nausithoos did, was decisive for establishing colonies; but to
make citizens land-owners was constitutive for every *polis* even in
mainland Greece. This process seems to have reached its end by the
8th century B.C., in contrast with the customs of wandering herdsmen
prevalent during migration periods and possibly the Indo-European
past.[35] As in sacrifice where the gods get their share first of all, the god
is also "princeps" in land division. The *temene* of the gods, with
borders clearly marked, are "taken out" and assigned as inalienable
property to their spiritual owners. The same is done with the *temene*
of heroes, those powerful dead who are now worshiped on behalf of
the whole city.[36] "Gods and heroes" are henceforth the two sets of
superior powers that are invoked in traditional cult and are presumed
to safeguard the city together; heroes, though, are secondary to the
gods and do not claim high-roofed "houses." As a city is bound to its
territory and people are bound to their city, the defense of the land
becomes the highest obligation of the citizen. *Polis* organization goes
hand in hand with a new military organization, especially hoplite
warfare. "Gods and heroes," themselves bound to their territory,
assume the function of highest legitimation in this context. Ever since
Tyrtaios the citizens are urged to fight "for the earth," for "gods and
heroes," while the gods are invoked to "break the spear" of the
aggressor (*Il.* 6,306) and expected to help in battle, even with direct

35. See Snodgrass 1977.

36. On the beginnings of hero cults, see J. N. Coldstream, "Hero-cults in the Age
of Homer," *Journal of Hellenic Studies* 96 (1976) 8–17; C. Bérard, "Récupérer la morte
du prince: héoisation et formation de la cité," and A. Snodgrass, "Les origines du culte
des héros dans la Grèce antique," *La mort, les morts dans les sociétés anciennes*
(eds. G. Gnoli and J.-P. Vernant; Cambridge: Cambridge University, 1982) 89–105,
107–19; Burkert 1985: 203–8.

epiphany. Thus the temples of the gods, visible from afar, nearly assume the role of a flag in battle, a background that gives confidence and feeling of security even in extreme danger.

This does not mean that temples must occupy the acropolis. We can distinguish at least three favorite sites for temples: at the height (*akra*), at the center (*agora*), and in marginal locations ("before the city," "in the marshes," etc.).[37] One may say that the acropolis is favored by Athena, the marketplace by Apollo—at Corinth, the heavy columns of the Apollo temple are still standing—and marginal areas by Artemis—a famous example is the Artemis temple of Kerkyra with the gorgon pediment. But the exceptions are too numerous to insist on rules. We may rather discern the traditional moves of worshipers to places of sacrifice, the "sacred routes" constituting later establishments which led to "high places" as well as to ponds or marshes for immersion sacrifice. The *prosodos* is prior to the *nāos*. A new direction is prescribed with the evolution of the *agora* as the true center of a *polis*: The "meeting place" becomes the economic center, the market. As contracts are made by oaths, accessible temples at the marketplace are necessary and become the most frequented. But it is all the temples taken together, in the pliable system of polytheism, that creates the identity of each individual *polis*.

The intimate connection of temple and *polis* is best seen in contrast with alternatives that are excluded by the *polis* system: if the temple is the distinctive and most prestigious building of a city, this reduces the significance of the palace, the castle, the town hall, and the monumental tomb, which in other civilizations played similar roles of distinction—Egyptian pyramids and Mycenaean tholoi, Minoan or Baroque palaces, Renaissance town halls. The *polis* is founded on the rejection of monarchy, on the common responsibility of autonomous equals who meet in the open air. If conservative Sparta retained the kings, entitled *archagetai*, their power was balanced by ephors, council, and *damos*. Elsewhere "God had become the monarch," as Viktor Ehrenberg put it.[38] In the case of Athens, it was Athena that was *archegetis*.[39] With regard to funerals, the intentional reduction of their elaborateness and significance is still documented at the beginning of the historical era. Common hero worship was installed instead.

One may still wonder at the precedence of the temple over the town hall, which might appear to be the more appropriate emblem of

37. See Polignac 1984.

38. V. Ehrenberg, *Der Staat der Griechen* (2d ed.; Zurich: Artemis, 1965) 19.

39. This title of the goddess of the Panathenaic festival appears in a new inscription, *Supplementum Epigraphicum Graecum* 28 (1978) 60, 65; cf. J. H. Kroll, "The Ancient Image of Athena Polias," *Hesperia Supplement* 20 (1982) 65–76.

a "city-state." Prestigious *bouleuteria* only arose in Hellenistic architecture. There were, of course, technical difficulties with larger rooms, but the Greeks did not even use existing temples for meetings of executive boards or delegates, as the Roman senate routinely did.[40] This avoidance of the temples for such meetings must have been based on a deep-rooted conviction that male activities are outdoor activities, be it sports, sacrifice, or decision-making in assemblies. The idea of "public," "political" space contrasts with "houses"; meetings in "houses" are for elite clubs only and are often viewed with suspicion. Group solidarity crystallizes in the open space in view of the divine, yet set apart from it. This leads back to the peculiar form of "Olympic" sacrifice: burning the bones "for the gods" on the altar with the temple at the back of the worshipers.

But this last statement brings us back to the basic question: why were the temples built at all? Why, on their way to a proto-democratic, proto-rational, humane society did the Greeks develop prestigious monuments of the superhuman? A possible answer that takes account of the social and economic dynamics may start from reflections on the ancient and widespread custom of "setting up" gifts for the gods. The efflorescence of votive gifts in the 8th century B.C., indicative of refined technology and economic growth in general, has been mentioned.[41] But there is more to it. To give something to a god means renunciation of the thing given; but as the gift is "set up" in a sanctuary, especially in durable forms like ceramics or metalwork, renunciation becomes demonstration of what is to stay. Through the invention of writing, even an individual's name can be preserved. In a way, sanctuaries are primarily public places designed for the display and preservation of *anathemata*.

Even as the distinction between cult image and votive image seemed to be unclear and not even very essential, so the whole temple, nay the whole acropolis of Athens, can be said to be one huge *anathema* to the divinity (Demosth. 22,76; Plut. *Per.* 12; 14). *Anathemata* are a form of display, of public show-off which, in contrast to other such forms, does not raise rivalry or envy because the objects are no longer private property, while remaining documents of pride and abiding fame. A temple is the most prestigious and lasting monument into which the available surplus of society is transformed—a monument of common identity. The factual permanence of the *anathema* in the sacred precinct corresponds to the idea of permanence and local stability on which the *polis* is based, with established

40. T. Mommsen, *Römisches Staatsrecht* (Leipzig: Hirzel, 1888), 3:926-31.
41. Cf. n. 29.

boundaries and the appeal to "ancestral custom." That which is beyond the reach of the individual—lasting success and stability—is
evoked in the abode of the divine. A Greek temple is the sumptuous
and beautiful *anathema* by which a *polis*, yielding to the divine,
demonstrates to herself and to others her existence and her claims. In
this way the tensions of a basically egalitarian, non-hierarchical, and
yet highly competitive society could find a creative outlet; the success
remains astounding.

This interpretation of a Greek temple as an emblem of collective
identity in the political and military system of the archaic epoch
should still leave room for the unpredictable realities of religious
experience. We have the statement of Plato that sanctuaries arose
where divine powers chose or happened to manifest themselves (*Leg.*
738c). The dimensions of anxiety, superstition, and faith that charac-
terize religion in its unforeseeable developments cannot and should
not be fully integrated in systems analysis.

Conclusion

There remains the connotation of art with the Greek temple, and
of the artificial. The temple is an *agalma*, a piece of pride and delight,
an incarnation of beauty, but also an emblem of wealth and power,
not to be separated from politics and prestige.

There are indications that the importance of temples decreased
with the decline of the Greek *polis*. Private dedications at the acropolis
of Athens are abundant down to the 5th century B.C. and become
scarce in later epochs. Few temples were built to the gods of Greece
after the 4th century B.C. It is also significant that temple building
readily accommodated itself to new and problematic trends: abstract
divinities, such as *Tyche*, 'Chance', and above all Hellenistic rulers
followed by the Roman emperors received their temples.[42] Here
again we may discern the function of a façade that may cover even
the void: they were monuments of prestige and honor rather than the
expression of spontaneous and sincere piety. It is still the cities that
decree the honors and build the monuments, even to the Roman
emperors. The cities of Asia Minor in particular competed for the
permission of the emperors to excel in ruler cult and to bear the title
of *neokoros*, 'temple-servant'; Smyrna led the ranks. Many other
temples decayed—witness the descriptions of Pausanias in the 2nd

42. See F. W. Hamdorf, *Griechische Kultpersonifikationen der vorhellenistischen
Zeit* (Mainz: Zabern, 1964); C. Habicht, *Gottmenschentum und griechische Städte*
(2d ed.; Munich: Beck 1970); S. R. F. Price, *Rituals and Power: The Roman Imperial
Cult in Asia Minor* (Cambridge: Cambridge University, 1984).

century A.D.—but others continued to function nevertheless, tended by conscientious citizens in the course of the traditional festivals, as long as some kind of Greek bourgoisie could socially and economically survive. When Christianity took over, the emperors were undecided for awhile whether to give the temples to the mobs for destruction or to preserve them[43] without their images as the prestigious façades to which the civilization had become accustomed for such a long time. But the museum functions of temples did not last.

What temple and image still meant to a pagan in the 5th century A.D. can be seen from the biography of Proklos, head of the Platonic Academy in Athens: he was happy that his house was in view of the "Acropolis of Athena," of the Parthenon; and when the chryselephantine statue of Pheidias that had been standing there for more than 800 years was finally transported to Constantinople—where it was soon to disappear—he dreamt that a beautiful woman came to announce to him that he should prepare his house, because "The Lady from Athens wishes to stay with you."[44] The loss of the image is balanced by an internal, spiritual presence of the divine; the sadness of dying paganism is assuaged by the conviction that temple and image are less needed than ever. In fact, Neoplatonism with its systems of metaphysical hierarchies was worlds away from naive anthropomorphism and from the plastic art of the classical epoch, and was thus closer to the Hagia Sophia than to the Parthenon. Temples were left in ruins, to be rediscovered by neopagan philhellenists.

43. See D. Metzler, "Oekonomische Aspekte des Religionswandels in der Spätantike: Die Enteignung der heidnischen Tempel seit Konstantin," *Hephaistos* 3 (1981) 27–40.
44. Marinos, *Vita Procli*, 29f. (this testimony is missing in J. Overbeck, *Die antiken Schriftquellen zur Geschichte der bildenden Künste bei den Griechen* [Leipzig: Engelmann, 1868]).

Reference List

Bergquist, B.
  1967   *The Archaic Greek Temenos: A Study of Structure and Function.*
          Lund: Gleerup.

Burford, A.
  1965   The Economics of Greek Temple Building. *Proceedings of the
          Cambridge Philological Society* 191: 21–34.

Burkert, W.
  1985   *Greek Religion: Archaic and Classical.* Oxford: Blackwell.

Coldstream, J. N.
1985   Greek Temples: Why and Where? Pp. 67–97 in *Greek Religion and Society*, ed. P. E. Easterling and J. V. Muir. Cambridge: Cambridge University.

Corbett, P. E.
1970   Greek Temples and Greek Worshippers. *Bulletin of the Institute of Classical Studies* 17: 149–58.

Drerup, E.
1969   *Griechische Baukunst in geometrischer Zeit*. Göttingen: Vandenhoeck & Ruprecht.

Funke, E.
1981   Götterbild. *Reallexikon für Antike und Christentum* 11: 659–828.

Gruben, G.
1984   *Die Tempel der Griechen*. 3d ed. Munich: Hirmer.

Kalpaxis, A. E.
1976   *Früharchaische Baukunst in Griechenland und Kleinasien*. Athens, n.p.

Mallwitz, A.
1981   Zur Architektur Griechenlands im 8. und 7. Jh. *Archäologischer Anzeiger*, 599–642.

Martini, W.
1986   Vom Herdhaus zum Peripteros. *Athenische Mitteilungen* 101: 23–36.

Mazarakis-Ainian, A.
1985   Contribution à l'étude de l'architecture religieuse grecque des âges obscurs. *L'Antiquité Classique* 54: 5–48.

Polignac, F. de.
1984   *La naissance de la cité grecque: Cultes, espaces et société VIIIe–VIIe siècles avant J.C.* Paris: La Découverte.

Scully, V.
1979   *The Earth, the Temple, and the Gods: Greek Sacred Architecture.* 2d ed. New Haven and London: Yale University.

Snodgrass, A. M.
1977   *Archaeology and the Rise of the Greek State.* Cambridge: Cambridge University.

Additional Bibliography

Bammer, A. *Architektur und Gesellschaft in der Antike: Zur Deutung baulicher Symbole.* 2d ed. Vienna: Böhlau, 1985.

Berve, H., and G. Gruben. *Greek Temples, Theatres and Shrines.* London: Thames and Hudson, 1963.

Bevan, E. *Holy Images: An Inquiry into Idolatry and Image-Worship in Ancient Paganism and in Christianity.* London: Allen and Unwin, 1940.

Coldstream, J. N. *Geometric Greece*. London: Benn, 1977.

_____. *Deities in Aegean Art before and after the Dark Age*. London: Bedford College, 1977.

Dinsmoor, W. B. *The Architecture of Ancient Greece: An Account of Its Historic Development*. London: Batsford, 1950.

Kähler, H. *Der griechische Tempel: Wesen und Gestalt*. Berlin: Mann, 1964.

Knell, H. *Grundzüge der griechischen Architektur*. Darmstadt: Wissenschaftliche Buchgesellschaft, 1980.

Krause, C. "Griechische Baukunst." Pp. 230-77 in *Die Griechen und ihre Nachbarn* (Propyläen Kunstgeschichte I), ed. K. Schefold. Berlin: Propyläen, 1967.

Martin, R. "Architektur." Pp. 3-17 and 169-231 in *Das archaische Griechenland 620-480 v. Chr.*, ed. J. Charbonneaux, R. Martin, and F. Villard. Munich: Beck, 1969.

_____. "Architektur." Pp. 3-96 in *Das klassische Griechenland 480-330 v. Chr.*, ed. J. Charbonneaux, R. Martin, and F. Villard. Munich: Beck, 1971.

_____. "Architektur." Pp. 3-94 in *Das hellenistische Griechenland 330-50 v. Chr.*, ed. J. Charbonneaux, R. Martin, and F. Villard. Munich: Beck, 1971.

Mussche, H. F., ed. *Griechische Baukunst II 1: Die Sakralbauten*. Leiden: Brill, 1968.

Nilsson, M. P. *Geschichte der griechischen Religion*, 2 vols. Munich: Beck, 1967.

Richard, H. *Vom Ursprung des dorischen Tempels*. Bonn: Habelt, 1970.

Schefold, K. "Neues vom klassischen Tempel." *Museum Helveticum* 14 (1957) 20-32.

Tomlinson, R. A. *Greek Sanctuaries*. London: Elek, 1976.

The Hindu Temple and Indian Society

C. J. FULLER

I SHALL BEGIN MY DISCUSSION of the relation between the Hindu temple and Indian society by briefly indicating the dimensions of this very large topic.[1] Temples of basically the same design as those which exist today first began to be built in the Gupta period (fourth–seventh centuries A.D.) or even a few centuries earlier, and although many aspects of Hinduism and Indian society are continuous over one-and-a-half millennia, many others not. Numerous changes in the religion of the Hindus have taken place, notably the great expansion of devotionalist Hinduism (*bhakti*), in which devotion to the god is accorded priority over ritualistic scrupulousness.[2] Equally major changes in Indian society have occurred, of which the most important in relation to temples has arguably been the preponderant displacement of Hindu kings by successively Muslim kings, the British colonial government, and finally the modern Indian state. In addition to change over time, regional variation is equally problematic for any attempt at generalization about Hindu temples and society. In different parts of India, different forms of Hinduism have been or are dominant, so that different deities, different styles of worship, as well as differences in the relative importance of temples within the total religious field need to be taken into account. And the connection between these variations and regional variations in social structure is more easily postulated than explained. Moreover, the category "Hindu temple" embraces a vast range of institutions. At one end are the enormous complexes

1. The classic work on the Hindu temple is Stella Kramrisch, *The Hindu Temple* (Calcutta: Calcutta University, 1946). A shorter, less technical account is George Michell, *The Hindu Temple: An Introduction to Its Meaning* (London: Paul Elek, 1977). Also useful are A. L. Basham, *The Wonder That Was India* (London: Fontana, 1971) 357–66, and P. S. Rawson, "Early Art and Architecture," chap. 15 in *A Cultural History of India* (ed. A. L. Basham; Oxford: Clarendon, 1975).

2. There are innumerable works on Hinduism and its history, and not even a small sample can be listed here. Basham, *Wonder That Was India*, chap. 7, and Basham, ed., *Cultural History*, chaps. 6–9, 18, and 26 are useful starting points and include bibliographies.

constructed particularly in south Indian cities, with their elaborate
liturgy, sizable staff, and frequently vast wealth; in the middle are the
more moderately sized temples found in towns throughout India; at
the other end are the often rudimentary and crude buildings or
shelters which house the deities' images in thousands of villages and
towns across the land, having at best one festival per year and a
couple of part-time priests.

Because I cannot cover all this ground, I have decided to concentrate my efforts on a small part of the field. As an anthropologist
whose own research experience has been fieldwork in a contemporary
temple and whose own competence is more in ethnography than
history, I have decided to focus on synchronic comparison rather than
historical evolution.

My work is mainly concerned with variation in the relation between the temple and the social structure: in particular, variation
between the form of that relation in the great city on the one hand
and the village on the other. This variation in the relation between the
temple and society is itself one aspect of the complex problem of
describing and analyzing Hinduism sociologically, and although this is
not the place to discuss that larger issue, it needs to be borne in mind
that temples, and what goes on in them, are but one part of Hinduism
as a whole. Much Hindu religious practice takes place in the home, or
in the fields or on the riverbanks; some Hindus hardly ever visit
temples at all and many certainly engage in as much religious activity
outside temples as in them. One important strand of the classical
Hindu tradition holds that the temple is truly oneself, an idea well-
expressed in a poem by the twelfth-century devotionalist poet
Basavaṇṇa. He wrote: "The rich will make temples for Śiva. What
shall I, a poor man, do? My legs are pillars, the body the shrine, the
head a cupola of gold."[3] Consequently, it is said, only the religiously
immature actually need to go to built temples, and this traditional
view is often invoked by those Hindus who prefer not to visit
temples—frequently, it must be noted, because in addition they dis-
like the atmosphere in them and the habits of their priests.

The purpose of these last remarks is to insist that it would be a
serious error to assume that the study of temples is the study of
Hinduism as a whole. It is all too easy to be misled by the spectacular
architecture and elaborate rituals of the larger temples into according
them disproportionate significance. Though all of us are, I am sure,
consciously aware of the problem, it is perhaps still worth observing
that a symposium dedicated to the comparative study of temples runs

3. A. K. Ramanujan, *Speaking of Śiva* (Harmondsworth: Penguin, 1973) 19.

the risk of, first, reifying and implicitly exaggerating the significance of temples; second, assuming unjustifiably that the category "temple" refers cross-culturally to a specifiable socio-religious entity;[4] and third, overlooking variations in their relative importance in different religions and societies.

Architecture and Worship

Let me now provide some descriptive material about Hindu temples, which must inevitably be simplified.[5] Hindu temples are of course dedicated to Hindu deities, and normally they contain images of those deities before whom worship is carried out. The inner sanctum of a Hindu temple is an enclosed cell-like chamber with only one entrance, and in this sanctum is the main image of the deity, usually a carved stone figure, except in temples of the great god Śiva, where there is instead a *liṅga*, an aniconic phallic emblem. The inner sanctum almost always has an antechamber, and in the very smallest temples— such as those rude structures found in many villages—the temple consists solely of the sanctum containing the image and the ante- chamber. However, many temples are far more elaborate. Around the basic structure are built further halls and corridors, and elaborate towers either over the sanctum itself (as in the classical north Indian style) or over the entrance gates (as in the south Indian style). Fre- quently, the temple is a multiple structure; in a Śiva temple, for instance, there are usually two sancta—one for the god and one for his wife—and in a Viṣṇu temple there may be three—since Viṣṇu has two wives.

Larger temples also contain many subsidiary images, housed in shrines or standing freely in the outer halls and corridors, and a proportion of these images will also be regular objects of worship. Large temples frequently include smaller separate temples within them as well. The great temple in Madurai, south India, dedicated to the goddess Mīnākṣī and her husband Sundareśvara (a form of Śiva), which I studied, is one of the great masterpieces of south Indian

4. This point was not readily accepted at the symposium. However, I would continue to appeal to the conventional wisdom of modern social and cultural anthro- pology, which has abandoned the positivistic chimera of cross-cultural analytical defini- tions, whether of "religion" or "family," "house" or "temple." To try to devise analytical distinctions between "temple," "church," "mosque," etc., is, to my mind, futile and liable to obscure most of the interesting and significant questions.

5. In my description of the temple and Hindu worship (and indeed throughout), I do not supply all the indigenous terms in order to avoid encumbering the text with numerous Sanskrit and other Indian words.

temple architecture.[6] It has two main sancta—one each for Mīnākṣī and Sundareśvara—which define its elaborated double structure, and it also contains a water-tank, in which worshipers can clean and purify themselves. A high wall surrounds the entire complex of buildings (which cover an area measuring 850 feet by 720 feet), and a series of lofty towers surmount the outer and inner gateways. Throughout the temple complex are subsidiary images of different forms of Śiva and the goddess, and other deities associated with them, and the total number of separate images which are at least occasionally objects of worship is around two hundred.

There are other temples in south India which compare in size with the Mīnākṣī Temple, but the vast majority of Hindu temples are considerably smaller. Nor do many of them attract as many worshipers as the Mīnākṣī Temple, which is visited by an average of approximately 20,000 people every day of the year, with Fridays—the day sacred to the goddess—normally drawing some 25,000. Irrespective of size or popularity, however, the fundamental plan is always the same and, as I have said, it minimally consists of an inner sanctum containing the image of the presiding deity and an antechamber.

The normal term for Hindu worship is *pūjā*. Once again, the forms of temple worship vary greatly, but all can be understood in terms of a basic modal pattern.[7] The fundamental premise is that the image contains the deity's power and worship before the image is worship of the deity whose power is within it. Worship comprises a series of services and offerings to the deity, such as bathing the image, dropping flowers on it, serving food before it or waving lamps in front of it. The theology implied and the interpretation of the meaning of *pūjā* are complicated matters on which there is scholarly disagreement. I should therefore warn that not all scholars would agree with my contention that the logic of Hindu worship does necessarily depend on a distinction between gods and their images— the gods being worshiped and not the images—and that the purpose of the services and offerings is not to provide for the needs of the deities, since they have none, but to act as if they had needs in order to demonstrate respect and devotion for them as their human servants. Such service to the deities is, I would argue, the fundamental raison d'être of worship in the temples, even if (as is the case) not all worshipers can articulate it in these terms. Worship is performed so

6. See C. J. Fuller, *Servants of the Goddess: The Priests of a South Indian Temple* (Cambridge: Cambridge University, 1984) esp. chap. 1.

7. Ibid., 10–22 and sources cited there; for an excellent interpretation taking a slightly different view, see Diana L. Eck, *Darśan: Seeing the Divine Image in India* (Chambersburg: Anima, 1981) chap. 2.

that the gods will protect their worshipers, either collectively or individually, and the world in which they all live, for example, by guaranteeing rainfall, the fertility of the soil, and the process of human reproduction. When carried out on behalf of the collectivity, temple worship is generally done by priests and other specialized ritual personnel; when carried out on behalf of individuals, who are seeking boons from the deities, it may be done by the priests or by individual worshipers themselves. Rules about whether a priest is required vary greatly between temples and between regions of India; for example, in north Indian temples devotees can often place their flowers on or food before the main images for themselves, whereas in the south they are frequently required to employ a priest.

Ideally, in all temples, worship of the deities should be done daily, but in small and neglected temples it may be done much less often, whereas in large and well-endowed temples like the Mīnākṣī Temple, there are eight periods every day at which worship before different images is carried out. In addition to the daily worship, there are regular cycles of worship determined by the week, lunar fortnight, lunar and solar months, and year, and in all temples the most spectacular ritual events tend to be the great festivals celebrated annually. In small temples, one annual festival is the most that anyone can expect; in large temples, every month may bring another annual festival, but invariably one of these is *the* great annual festival, the climax of the temple's year. Broadly speaking, therefore, we can again speak of a basic cycle of regular worship, the elaboration of which varies greatly but is always guided by the same elementary template of periodicities.

Brahmanical and non-Brahmanical Temples

Although all Hindu temples do have features in common, the literature conventionally distinguishes between Brahmanical temples dedicated to Sanskritic or "great tradition" deities, and non-Brahmanical temples dedicated to non-Sanskritic or "little tradition" or village deities. In the former, the priests are Brahmans who serve the classical, pan-Indian deities, mainly—in one form or another—Viṣṇu, Śiva, and the goddess Devī. The liturgical language in these temples is mainly Sanskrit and the food offerings made during worship are almost always purely vegetarian. All towns and cities in India contain Brahmanical temples of one kind or another, and they are also found in many villages, especially those in which a sizable proportion of the population belongs to Brahman or other high-ranking castes. In the non-Brahmanical temples, the priests come from lower-ranking non-Brahman castes, and the gods worshiped are the so-called "village deities" (*grāma devatā*), a variety of gods and more especially goddesses who tend to be more identified with particular localities. The vernacular languages are used in ritual and although worship with vegetarian food offerings is still an ubiquitous feature, meat offerings and animal sacrifices are common as well. All villages contain temples to the village deities, but the term is misleading because these temples are universally found in urban settlements as well.

Hindu society is famous for its hierarchical caste system, in which the highest rank is occupied by the Brahmans and the lowest by the Untouchables or Harijans. Modern anthropologists of India have devoted much of their attention to studying the caste system and the most outstanding theoretical work in Indian anthropology is undoubtedly Dumont's book, *Homo Hierarchicus*, which attempts to show that the structure of Hindu society is defined by the religious ideology of hierarchy.[8] Dumont's book, for reasons I need not discuss now, actually says practically nothing about temples or worship of the gods, but the centrality of hierarchy in his theory is also characteristic of much work on Hinduism done in the 1950s and 1960s, which attempts to show how the division between Sanskritic and non-Sanskritic deities reflects in the religious sphere the social hierarchy of caste. The Sanskritic deities are seen as higher-ranking than the non-Sanskritic deities, as is notably marked by their Brahman as opposed to non-Brahman priests, their language of worship (Sanskrit rather than the vernacular), and their vegetarian versus non-vegetarian diet. In other words, to sum up the approach very simply, the Hindu religion is understood as a kind of Durkheimian reflection of society— a hierarchical society must logically have a homologously hierarchical divinity and religion.[9]

For a variety of reasons, this relatively direct application of the Durkheimian approach, in which the classification of deities mirrors classification by rank in the social system, can be shown to run into insuperable difficulties. In concluding this paper, I shall try to show that the Sanskritic versus non-Sanskritic distinction, which originally derives from Srinivas, is connected to the social structure in a more

8. Louis Dumont, *Homo Hierarchicus: The Caste System and Its Implications* (London: Weidenfeld and Nicolson, 1970).

9. E.g., Louis Dumont, "A Structural Definition of a Folk Deity of Tamil Nad: Aiyanar, the Lord," in *Religion, Politics and History in India* (Paris: Mouton, 1970); Edward B. Harper, "Ritual Pollution as an Integrator of Caste and Religion," *Journal of Asian Studies* 23 (1964) 151-97; for critique, C. J. Fuller, "Gods, Priests and Purity: On the Relation Between Hinduism and the Caste System," *Man* 14 (1979) 459-76.

mediated and complex way.[10] Here, however, I must identify some of the most crucial objections to the more straightforward Durkheimian postulate.

First, although Hindus themselves do make categorical distinctions broadly equivalent to Sanskritic versus non-Sanskritic deities, these distinctions have to be understood as ideological, because it is actually impossible to classify unambiguously Hindu deities, in terms of their putative attributes, with reference to such distinctions. Indeed, it is a principal feature of the pantheon that, for example, both Sanskritic and non-Sanskritic deities are often explicitly understood to be forms of each other and are so represented in myth and ritual.[11]

Second, although it is true that Brahmans are the highest caste, Brahman priests are actually the most lowly and even degraded and despised of Brahmans, so that the ostensible correlation between the high rank of Sanskritic deities and the high rank of their priests breaks down.[12] Much other evidence also undermines the argument that there is a caste hierarchy among the gods which can be directly linked to that of humans, for example, the evidence on food transactions between gods and humans as opposed to between humans only.[13]

Third, the narrow emphasis on hierarchy and caste ranking means that other obviously significant aspects of Hinduism are ignored or unproductively forced into a Procrustean framework inhibiting holistic interpretation. Once serious and detailed research work began on Hindu temples, it rapidly became clear that what we might label caste-centered Durkheimianism was an inadequate methodological tool for their analysis.

Temples and Kings

One significant legacy of Dumont's theory of caste hierarchy is a fundamental misapprehension of the role of the traditional Hindu

10. M. N. Srinivas, *Religion and Society Among the Coorgs of South India* (Oxford: Clarendon, 1952); cf. Srinivas, *Social Change in Modern India* (Berkeley: University of California, 1966) chap. 1, "Sanskritization"; cf. J. F. Staal, "Sanskrit and Sanskritization," *Journal of Asian Studies* 22 (1963) 261–75. The distinction is similar but not identical to the "great" versus "little tradition" distinction: Robert Redfield and Milton Singer, "The Cultural Role of Cities," *Economic Development and Cultural Change* 3 (1954) 53–73; McKim Marriott, "Little Communities in an Indigenous Civilization," *Village India* (ed. M. Marriott; Chicago: University of Chicago, 1969) 191–218.

11. Marriott, "Little Communities," illustrates this clearly.

12. Fuller, *Servants of the Goddess*, chap. 3 and sources cited there.

13. Gabriella Eichinger Ferro-Luzzi, "The Food of the Gods Versus Human Food in South India," *L'Uomo* 5 (1981) 239–66; Fuller, "Gods, Priests and Purity," 470–71.

king. The king, for Dumont, is essentially a secular political figure and his authority is consequently perceived as non-religious.[14] Studies of temples by anthropologists, historians, and religious scholars rapidly showed that this picture of Hindu kingship did not make much sense and because much of the most interesting work on temples done over the last decade or so has focused on the theme of kingship, this is the best place to begin.[15] It is probably most fruitful to outline here a synthetic approach, one which emphasizes academic consensus rather than disputation, but I should make it clear that this synthesis is mine. It is not one which would necessarily meet the approval of other scholars in the field upon whose work I shall be drawing. In particular, I shall largely ignore significant differences in approach between what we could label the American and French schools.

The most useful initial signpost is perhaps Stein's concept of "shared sovereignty," the idea that sovereignty is shared between deity and king.[16] The significance of the notion that the deity is or is like a king has long been recognized; gods are, for example, often addressed as monarchs, the ritual of worship in temples has much in common with the presentation of homage to human kings, and temples are often equated with palaces. The temple and the palace are, as Biardeau puts it, the double center of the kingdom,[17] although Stein suggests that in the medieval period the south Indian temple

14. Dumont, "The Conception of Kingship in Ancient India," in *Religion, Politics and History in India*.

15. E.g., Arjun Appadurai, *Worship and Conflict Under Colonial Rule: A South Indian Case* (Cambridge: Cambridge University, 1981); Arjun Appadurai and Carol A. Breckenridge, "The South Indian Temple: Authority, Honor and Redistribution," *Contributions to Indian Sociology* 10 (1976) 187-211; Madeleine Biardeau, *L'Hindouisme: Anthropologie d'une civilisation* (Paris: Flammarion, 1981); Nicholas B. Dirks, "Political Authority and Structural Change in Early South Indian History," *Indian Economic and Social History Review* 13 (1976) 125-57; "The Structure and Meaning of Political Relations in a South Indian Little Kingdom," *Contributions to Indian Sociology* 13 (1979) 169-204; *The Hollow Crown: Ethnohistory of an Indian Kingdom* (Cambridge: Cambridge University, forthcoming); Fuller, *Servants of the Goddess*; "Royal Divinity and Human Kingship in the Festivals of a South Indian Temple," *South Asian Social Scientist* 1 (1985) 3-43; Jean-Claude Galey, ed., "L'espace du temple," part 1, *Purusartha* 8 (1985) and part 2, *Purusartha* 10 (1986); Anncharlott Eschmann, Hermann Kulke, and Gaya Charan Tripathi, eds., *The Cult of Jagannath and the Regional Tradition of Orissa* (New Delhi: Manohar, 1978) chaps. 7, 8, 11, 17 and 18; Marie-Louise Reiniche, *Les dieux et les hommes: étude des cultes d'un village du Tirunelveli, Inde du Sud* (Paris: Mouton, 1979); Burton Stein, *Peasant State and Society in Medieval South India* (Delhi: Oxford University, 1980).

16. Burton Stein, "Introduction," to *South Indian Temples: An Analytical Reconsideration* (ed. B. Stein; New Delhi: Vikas, 1978) 7.

17. Biardeau, *L'Hindouisme*, 20.

may itself have been a fortified place and thus not clearly separate from other royal, military edifices.[18] Conversely, the Hindu king, while not necessarily being regarded explicitly as divine, was or is normally held to be either an incarnation or descendant of a god, or an embodiment of divine powers, or an earthly representative of the gods. In the classical Hindu world view, an ordered society is predicated on kingship, and kingship is undoubtedly the first key to appreciating the relation between the Hindu temple and society.

A principal duty of the traditional Hindu king was protection of his realm, of the land and its peoples and the institutions therein, including the temples. (I use the past tense because no Hindu king still officially rules in India, although in some regions the erstwhile maharajas do perform some of their ancient functions even today.) However, this protection could not be provided only by what we would now identify as secular governmental action, since the traditional Hindu king (like the traditional king in so many societies) was simultaneously a political and religious figure. Thus protection of the kingdom required the king to sustain the proper relationship between himself and the gods (of whom, as we have seen, he was generally regarded as one or another type of incarnation or delegate), so that the kingdom—itself conceived of as a microcosm of the world and universe—continued to receive the divine protection imperative for its survival and prosperity. There were numerous ways in which the royal duty of protection had to be discharged, but one of them was the protection of temples, the sites in which so many rituals for the collective benefit of the kingdom were conducted. This did not just mean that the king had to ensure that temple buildings were maintained; it also meant that, at least in principle, the king was responsible for ensuring that rituals were correctly carried out by appointing competent priests and other personnel, by arranging adequate funding to meet ritual expenses, and by intervening as the deities' representative to settle disputes in the temple which threatened any misperformance of rituals. If all this were done, then one crucial guarantor of the kingdom's prosperity was ensured; if it was not, then disaster threatened and, at least in south Indian ritual texts, it was normally stated that catastrophe would first strike the king, and then his subjects at large.[19]

Empirically, the king probably normally involved himself directly only in the affairs of the great temples in his realm, and especially of

18. Burton Stein, "Towns and Cities: The Far South," *The Cambridge Economic History of India* (ed. Tapan Raychaudhuri and Irfan Habib; Cambridge: Cambridge University, 1982), 1:456–57.

19. Fuller, *Servants of the Goddess*, 203, n. 55.

the major temples in his capital city which were dedicated to the
kingdom's tutelary deity. The Mīnākṣī Temple in Madurai was such a
temple, and it is clear that the Nāyaka kings of the sixteenth to
seventeenth centuries were actively involved in the appointment of
priests, the settlement of disputes between them, the granting of tax-
free land to priests and other temple staff, the establishment of
endowments (again with land grants) to pay for rituals and for upkeep
of the temple fabric, as well as the inauguration of new rituals and
festivals (or the revival of old ones) paid for by those endowments.
The Nāyaka kings also played a part in some of the rituals themselves,
notably those celebrating the coronations of Mīnākṣī and Sundareśvara,
the original and eternal monarchs of Madurai. These rituals served to
demonstrate publicly the shared sovereignty of the human and divine
kings.[20]

On the evidence available, it appears that a broadly similar role
in the activities and rituals of their kingdoms' major temples was
played by the Hindu kings of the past over much of India,[21] although
it should of course be recalled that Muslims, not Hindus, governed
vast tracts of the country for several centuries before the onset of
colonial rule. One consequence of this historical fact is that researchers
particularly interested in Hindu temples have been inclined to work in
regions where Hindu traditions have been ostensibly less affected by
the Muslim impact, so that there is remarkably sparse information
available on temples in much of northern India. We therefore know
rather little about them in the vast Gangetic plain, which paradoxically
was not only the heartland of the Mughal empire, but is also the
region in which Benares and other major Hindu holy cities are located.
In these cities, which are above all else pilgrimage centers on the
River Ganges, it does in fact look as if temples were probably less
central than they were in, say, the southern cities. Particularly striking,
for instance, is that the hub of Benares is its cremation grounds on the
riverbank, not Śiva's Viśvanātha temple, even though that temple is
generally regarded throughout India as the god's holiest shrine.[22] I
ought therefore to make it clear that my generalizations in this lecture
are not equally based on evidence from all of India and are actually
rather heavily dependent on material from the south, where so much
of the research has been carried out.

20. Ibid., chap. 4, "Royal Divinity and Human Kingship."
21. Cf. references cited in n. 15 above.
22. Jonathan Parry, "Death and Cosmogony in Kashi," *Contributions to Indian
Sociology* 15 (1981) 337–65; Diana L. Eck, *Banaras: City of Light* (London: Routledge &
Kegan Paul, 1984) 120–36 on Viśvanātha; cf. Fuller, *Servants of the Goddess*, 70–71.

Kingship, Sacrifice, and Gifts

The paradigms of modern social science naturally lead us to interpret the king's role in the temples in terms of legitimation, i.e., the power of a ruler is here turned into the legitimate authority of a king by representing its source as divine. Since the general concept of traditional political authority as dependent upon religious legitimation will be familiar, I hardly need to explicate it here; nor shall I try to deny that legitimation is a key process in this context. However, it is highly pertinent that in relation to the paradigms of traditional Hindu ideology itself the concept of religious legitimation is misplaced. The king's role in the temple does not buttress or mystify his political role; it is itself a constitutive element of his role. The Hindu king is, in a vital respect, only a true king insofar as he does place himself in a proper relationship with the gods and therefore does ensure that the order of the cosmos and the kingdom is preserved, the precondition for the survival and prosperity of his kingdom and people.[23]

From within the indigenous tradition, the king, in his relation to the temples and the deities within them, can be seen as the continuation, but also the transformation, of the classical *yajamāna*, the patron of the ancient Vedic sacrifice. (The Vedic religion of ca. 1500–500 b.c. was not only the historical forerunner of modern Hinduism; it also defines, for the Hindus, the authoritative source and unchanging form of their religion.) The Vedic patron provided the wherewithal for the sacrifice and was the recipient of its fruits; the ritual acts themselves, however, were the responsibility of the priests whose remuneration was met by the patron.

As several writers have shown, worship in the Hindu temple can correspondingly be understood as a structural transformation of the classical Vedic sacrifice, although the degree of transformation of both the patron's role and the rite itself is a subject of considerable dispute. Whereas some authors stress the continuities underlying the transformations, others argue that the continuities can really only be treated as pious fictions.[24] However, one important transformation

23. "Il serait inadmissible que la fonction royale, si centrale dans le maintien de l'ordre social, ne fût pas pleinement intégrée à l'ordre socio-cosmique, au dharma, qui unit le ciel et la terre, les dieux et les hommes" (Biardeau, *L'Hindouisme*, 63).

24. Biardeau particularly stresses the continuity; see especially, "Le sacrifice dans l'Hindouisme," *Le sacrifice dans l'Inde ancienne* (ed. M. Biardeau and Charles Malamoud; Paris: Universitaires de France, 1976) 139–54 and passim; cf. also Reiniche, *Les dieux et les hommes*. J. C. Heesterman particularly argues against continuity; see especially, *The Inner Conflict of Tradition* (Chicago: University of Chicago, 1985) chap. 6.

especially relevant to this discussion is the primacy which came to be
accorded, at least in south India, to the king's role as a donor, the
ultimate giver to the deities in the temple, as well as to the officiants
responsible for the rituals. In other words, as inscriptional evidence
best reveals, the medieval Hindu king's function at the temple came
to be represented, in certain contexts anyway, as that of a donor
rather than of a sacrificer.[25] Whether gift-giving, which is regularly
assimilated into the category of sacrifice in classical Hindu thought,
should therefore be treated as continuous with sacrifice or as a distinct
transformation of it, is precisely the interpretative dilemma to which I
have just referred and intend to circumvent. However, I may as well
mention that contemporary American scholars (such as Appadurai,
Dirks, or Stein) have particularly stressed the primary role of gifting,
whereas French scholars (such as Reiniche, strongly influenced by
Biardeau) have been more inclined to stress the role of the sacrificial
patron and therefore to see gifting as but one expression of his
classical function.[26] Other writers, like myself, have tended to com-
promise by drawing on both approaches.

Trying to understand the king's role from within indigenous
ideology does not merely reflect an intellectual desire to represent the
culturally other as accurately as possible; it is also a prerequisite for
a proper grasp of Hindu kingship as a political and religious phenomenon. In particular, it has been argued—most prominently by
Stein—that the medieval Hindu king's *political* role (using that term in
its usual Western sense to refer to real power over human and material
resources) was actually much less focal than most historians have
tended to assume.[27] Thus, for example, inscriptional panegyrics to
royal overlords do not necessarily indicate real political suzerainty,
but rather ritual suzerainty in the sense that only a grant made in the
king's name was held to be valid. Thus if a local chieftain made gifts
to the deities in his local temple, he invoked the king's name because—
to compress a complex argument—only a royal gift served to re-
produce the proper ordering of the cosmos and kingdom.

Local Temples and "Little Kings"

The question of when a chieftain is or is not a king raises another
thicket of problems. However, it leads on to the next vital point,

25. Dirks, "Political Authority and Structural Change."
26. Cf. references cited in nn. 15 and 16, and Marie-Louise Reiniche, "Le temple
dans la localité: quatre exemples au Tamilnad," *Purusartha* 8 (1985) 75–119, for a
critique of Appadurai and the Americans on pp. 81–84 and 112–14.
27. *Peasant State and Society,* passim.

which is that a local chieftain and indeed a village headman must, as has long been recognized, be seen as a "little king."[28] The little kingdom of the chieftainship or village is a microcosmic homologue of the great kingdom, and the little king has a function in relation to his subjects homologous with that of the great king, in whose name (and sometimes by whose delegation) he acts authoritatively. Moreover, the little king then shares sovereignty with the deities in his local temple as the great king shares it with the deities in the great royal temples of the cities.

Political communities are therefore, in Stein's words, communities of worship, defined by their common recognition of a particular shared sovereignty—whether at the level of the village (or some other local caste- or kin-based unit) or at the level of the kingdom as a whole.[29] Thus, if the Nāyaka king of Madurai was the principal sacrificial patron and donor in relation to Mīnākṣī and Sundareśvara, so the headman of a village in, say, the remoter marches of the kingdom was homologously the patron and donor of, for instance, his village's tutelary goddess. Further, since others besides the king or little king can and do make donations to the gods, these donors must also be regarded as subordinate participants in the role of patron-cum-donor, so that the king's function is actually shared by some of his subjects.

As just mentioned, a considerable amount of recent scholarship on the Hindu temple has explored the significance of gifting. In the great urban temples, donations are and were normally made in the form of endowments, trusts deriving their income from (usually) a land grant, which meets the expenses of certain specified rituals. In principle, each and every ritual (or component of a ritual) is the responsibility of a particular endowment, so that the temple as a whole is a "radically decentralized organization."[30] No one, not even the king, actually controls all the resources of the temple, but the king does have the crucial role of settling disputes between donors or endowment trustees. Such disputes seem to have been frequent, and tended to erupt over the issue of honors. At the conclusion of a ritual sponsored by a particular donor, that person is entitled to receive from the deity, at the hands of the priest, an honor (for example, a silk cloth tied around the head). The value and style of honors, the order in which they are given, and the identity of the recipient are

28. The seminal statements are Bernard S. Cohn, "Political Systems in Eighteenth Century India: The Banaras Region," *Journal of the American Oriental Society* 82 (1962) 312–20; Dumont, *Homo Hierarchicus,* chap 7.

29. Stein, "Introduction" in *South Indian Temples,* 7–8.

30. Appadurai and Breckenridge, "The South Indian Temple," 202.

and probably always have been causes of immense potential acrimony, not infrequently so severe that rituals could be brought to a complete halt until they were sorted out.[31]

In my opinion, there has been a tendency in some of the literature to extend the analysis of honors too far. Thus the relationship between the deity and the donor receiving the honors has been incorrectly seen as the paradigm of all significant relationships in the temple, including those between the deity and ritual officiants or ordinary devotees, which are in fact quite differently constituted, although I do not want to pursue this specialists' argument here.[32] More relevant, perhaps, is that the above sketch of the traditional honors system in the great temple is only partly applicable to the contemporary situation, because there is usually no longer a king to settle disputes. Innumerable quarrels arising in temples have ended up in law courts and the development of the law has itself had a major impact on the organization of temples and religious endowments. Since the days of the British, modern governments have also massively intervened in the affairs of many temples across India.[33] Unfortunately, though, this vast and fascinating topic will have to be ignored here, for now I must turn to the small rural temples.

In these small temples, endowments of the king found at major temples are less important. They do exist and often, for example, the basic income of a small temple and the remuneration of its priest come from a plot of donated land effectively controlled by the family whose ancestors first made the gift. However, the sponsorship of these small temples' festivals is often met by collecting money or provisions as and when these are required, and it is common for such collections to be made according to a typical pattern. For instance, if the festival of a deity of a clan or caste group is being celebrated, then all members of the clan or group are expected to contribute and each family will probably be expected to take a specific role in the festival itself. The headman, the little king, will be the patron of the festival and he is likely to preside at its climax; he may, for instance, be responsible for supplying the animal to be immolated at this time if, as is common, an animal sacrifice is required by the deity in question. In the case of a festival for the tutelary goddess of a village, a standard pattern is for different caste groups in the village to be responsible for different days' activities and again for the village

31. Appadurai, *Worship and Conflict*, chap 1; Appadurai and Breckenridge, "The South Indian Temple"; Dirks, *Hollow Crown*, chap. 13.

32. Cf. Fuller, *Servants of the Goddess*, chap. 2.

33. See, e.g., Appadurai, *Worship and Conflict*; Fuller, *Servants of the Goddess*, chaps. 4–6.

headman, or the headman of the village's dominant caste, to take the presiding role at the festival's climax. Honors similar to those distributed at major temples are also a frequent feature of these smaller temple festivals, if on a less elaborate scale.[34]

On the whole, I think it is fair to say that most of the best recent scholarship—in anthropology, history, and Indology—has emphasized the continuities and similarities between the temples of the great cities and small villages, between great kings and little kings and their respective shared sovereignties, and between the deities enshrined in the different types of temples. The guiding paradigm is the macrocosm encompassing the microcosm, with each small-scale formation seen as a homologous microcosm of each large-scale formation. This paradigm has proved invaluable in analysis and has helped to clear away many obstructive misapprehensions deriving originally from outdated, ethnocentric assumptions about Aryan and autochthonous deities, or unstable empires and sempiternal village republics. Nevertheless, I believe that the emphasis on continuities has now begun to be overstated and that there are salient and significant differences between temples and their respective relations to society which need to be investigated. In the last section of this paper, I shall briefly scan this area, which I have begun to investigate in my own researches.

Community and Deity Festivals

Throughout India, as I stated earlier, Hindus do make broadly dichotomous distinctions between deities. The anthropological categories of "Sanskritic" and "non-Sanskritic" can justifiably be employed to label these distinctions.[35] Ethnographic evidence shows that such distinctions are drawn differently in different regions of India, and are

34. This paragraph presents a synthetic picture, which is not a description of any specific case, but is abstracted from a range of sources: Brenda E. F. Beck, *Peasant Society in Konku* (Vancouver: University of British Columbia, 1972) 79–100, 110–21, 141–43; R. L. Brubaker, "Barbers, Washermen and Other Priests: Servants of the South Indian Village and Its Goddess," *History of Religions* 19 (1979) 128–52; Louis Dumont, *Une sous-caste de l'Inde du sud: organisation sociale et religion des Pramalai Kallar* (Paris: Mouton, 1957) part 3; Anthony Good, "The Annual Goddess Festival in a South Indian Village," *South Asian Social Scientist* 1 (1985) 119–67; Olivier Herrenschmidt, "Le Sacrifice du buffle en Andhra côtier," *Purusartha* 5 (1981) 133–77; "Quelles fêtes pour quelles castes?" *L'Homme* 22 (1982) 31–55; Reiniche, *Les dieux et les hommes*, 86–92, 119–20, 136–46, 150–61, 170–82; Srinivas, *Religion and Society*, 177–212.

35. I have in mind a justification akin to that of J. A. B. van Buitenen, "On the Archaism of the *Bhāgavata Purāṇa*," *Krishna: Myths, Rites and Attitudes* (ed. Milton Singer; Chicago: University of Chicago, 1968) 34–35, on "Sanskritic" as standing for an indigenous value.

also drawn differently by, say, Hindus of higher and lower castes, or by urban dwellers and villagers. It is therefore an oversimplification to assume that "Sanskritic" and "non-Sanskritic" always have the same referents, and it is the conceptual dichotomy itself which is significant, rather than the "content" of the two categories. In addition, as I also mentioned before, all attempts to classify deities unequivocally into one or other such category by reference to their putative attributes have persistently foundered, for the distinctions in question are not in fact descriptively accurate, whatever Hindu informants may claim. The recognition that this is so has itself been a major stimulus to the contemporary emphasis on continuities. The problem, however, is that because Hindus themselves do make distinctions between their deities, even if they cannot adequately apply them to the perceived empirical facts, we cannot simply dismiss them as irrelevant; they are in reality part of the actors' own conceptual framework and this should caution us against over-enthusiastic adoption of the paradigm of homologous continuities. In other words—and this point I wish to stress—the Sanskritic versus non-Sanskritic distinction (in one guise or another) is a significant ideological or cultural construct of the Hindus themselves. That it is not an accurate descriptive scheme is true, but the distinction is nonetheless more than a mere mystification because, as I shall now try to show, it is demonstrably connected with variation in the ritually manifested relationship between the gods and society.

My argument is briefly as follows.[36] As I have just stated, ethnographic evidence on the organization of festivals celebrated for deities in villages, notably tutelary goddesses in south India, commonly reveals that each caste group in the community and each important officeholder is expected to sponsor and participate in a particular segment of the festival, and the village headman takes the presiding role. He is the little king who is shown to share his sovereignty with the goddess, and he is also the principal patron-cum-donor as representative of the village, though he also shares this role with the other groups and officeholders who participate. The village is thus revealed in the festival as a community of worshipers recognizing a particular shared sovereignty, and the ritual as a whole accords quite closely with a classical anthropological notion of ritual, also owed principally to Durkheim, as the expression or creator of social solidarity; in this case, of course, it is an organic solidarity based on a hierarchical division of ritual labor.

If we look at the festivals in a large temple like the Mīnākṣī Temple, the picture is different. In the past, the king did participate in

36. For more details, see Fuller, "Royal Divinity and Human Kingship."

some festivals himself and festivals focusing on the theme of kingship particularly expressed his shared sovereignty. The king also shared his donor's role with other subordinate endowment trustees. However, the available data suggest that in the Nāyaka period all or almost all these other donors were in one way or another connected with the royal house, so that it was not the community as a whole, but only its royal elite which actively participated in the festival. Thus the axis of the kingdom appeared on the ritual stage, but not the periphery since practically none of the kingdom's subjects were really involved. The village deity's festival represents a community of worshipers, but by the same token it also draws a boundary around that community and excludes non-members; the Mīnākṣī Temple festival, by contrast, fails to define such a community, but it also thereby draws no boundaries and excludes nobody. Anyone, potentially, can recognize the shared sovereignty displayed in the Mīnākṣī Temple. Thus Mīnākṣī and Sundareśvara are portrayed as reigning over a limitless realm and transcending any specifiable social unit, whereas their counterparts in the village are embedded in local communities and are indeed partially conceptualized as restricted to them. It is, for instance, one of the distinguishing characteristics of non-Sanskritic deities that they are primarily connected with a particular community and territory, so that their power is believed to extend only or mainly over that particular social space. Conversely, no such limits are normally held to apply to the power of Sanskritic deities, whose domain is the entire universe. The contrast between the domains of power of the two types of deity, I would argue, is clearly represented in rituals (as it is in myths, as Shulman's work shows)[37] and indeed it is to a large extent a function of the rituals. After all, gods are as they are mainly owing to how they reveal themselves in their rituals and associated myths. In other words, my contention is that the variable relation between the deity and the social structure as displayed ritually does itself underpin in social action the ideological construct by which the Hindus classify their deities.

Conclusion

Such a brief comparative sketch based on such a narrow range of evidence cannot by itself be treated as conclusive, and I have considerably simplified the picture in order to highlight the contrast. Nonetheless, I would suggest that the older anthropological approach,

---

37. David D. Shulman, *Tamil Temple Myths* (Princeton: Princeton University, 1980) esp. chap. 2.

which took as its starting point a Sanskritic versus non-Sanskritic distinction, was not quite as mistaken as recent scholars, seeking more unifying paradigms, have often assumed. Invaluable though the focus on kingship and the break with caste-centered theories have been, it is now time to look again at variation and to recognize that distinctions between deities, and their temple cults, are significant features of our data. All relations postulated between gods and society are themselves socio-cultural constructs, but the variation revealed here is one in which the gods are sometimes shown to be more closely linked to society and sometimes shown to transcend it. How the Hindus themselves represent the link between gods and society requires more investigation before we can make further progress in generating a better theoretical argument about that relation from the external, analytical point of view. The need for more investigation should not, however, be used as an excuse for refusing to think comparatively outside the Hindus' own categories, as some recent work has tended to do.

In presenting these conclusions, I have treated the relation between temples and society as a dependent variable which is itself constitutive of the relation between deities and society, and I have thus said rather less about temples themselves than I might have done. But the shift in emphasis does not, I hope, need any elaborate justification. Temples may be visible to us as built structures, but they should not be reified as misplaced concrete phenomena; for the Hindus, they are but one of the places in which worship of the deities takes place and it is of course the deities, not the temples themselves, who lie at the center of the religion and should therefore be the principal focus of our attempts to understand the significance of temples in India.

Mesoamerican Temples

GARY M. FEINMAN

RECENTLY, RICHARD BLANTON AND I (1984) argued that pre-Columbian Mesoamerica was in large part defined and interconnected by the trade and movement of luxury items and precious materials. This interpretation contrasts with Wallerstein's (1974) conception of pre-industrial Europe as a macro-region linked by the utilitarian exchanges of food and fuel. We also suggested that in ancient Mesoamerica many of these exotic raw materials and labor-intensive finished goods, such as cotton and textiles, shell, cocoa, gems, metal, and decorated ceramic vessels, were recognized as making symbolic statements about the purity and power of their owners (Blanton et al. 1981: 245–46). Furthermore, we noted that many sacred concepts, their physical representations, rituals, and cult figures (such as the feathered serpents, lords of the underworld, and spirits of rain-lightning; Blanton et al. 1981: 247–48), as well as blood-letting, human sacrifice, ancestor veneration, and funeral rituals, were pan-regional, understood by the elite across Mesoamerica. Thus, as I developed an interest in understanding what defined the spatial extent of ancient Mesoamerica (interconnecting the diverse polities and peoples of the Mesoamerican world), I grew to accept Thomas A. Lee's (1978: 2) statement that "since one of the characteristics of Mesoamerica is its surprisingly uniform religion it might be expected that religion could have been important in the establishment and maintenance of communication and cultural contact throughout the area."

During the last decade, interest and information about pre-Columbian religion, and particularly temples, also has been fostered by significant excavations at the Aztec Templo Mayor in downtown Mexico City by Mexico's National Institute of Anthropology and History. Begun in 1978 after the chance discovery (by an electrical worker) of a carved stone two meters below the street, the major horizontal uncovering of ancient Tenochtitlan's Great Temple has provided archaeologists with a basic plan of the edifice, how it was enhanced during the years prior to the Conquest, as well as additional insight into temple activities and ritual (Matos Moctezuma 1984a). Since archaeological findings have been complemented by 16th-century Spanish narratives describing the temple, our picture is more complete than that from most other Mesoamerican temples for which we are dependent on the archaeological record alone. Yet compared to the wealth of information on ancient Old World temples, even data on 16th-century Mesoamerican temples remain relatively sparse. The quality of the ancient Mesoamerican record cannot match the detailed richness that we have from regions where more voluminous historical materials have survived.

Clearly, the Templo Mayor, whose twin sanctuaries towered over the Central Precinct of Mesoamerica's largest and most powerful Conquest-era city, was not typical of pre-Columbian temples in size, grandeur, or importance. And indeed, it is somewhat deceptive, and troublesome, to present a single picture of the temple from any region. Yet through contextual comparisons of this relatively well-documented Central Mexican case with a broader spatial and temporal sample of Mesoamerican temples, more general properties of this pre-Hispanic institution can be seen. On a similar theme, Joyce Marcus (1983: 232) has noted previously "that the plan of the temples is one of the least varied and most conservative of all Mesoamerican features from region to region, being far more predictable than the form of the palace, the plan of the city, or the degree of urban concentration of craft specialists." Although space/time variation in Mesoamerican temples will not be ignored, the principal focus here is on general features, to facilitate a comparison of this pre-Columbian institution with the temple in other pre-industrial domains.

The Plan of the Temple

Archaeologists too often have tended to identify as a temple any structure that is both non-residential and incompletely understood. I have tried to avoid this trap by adopting a rather conservative definition of the Mesoamerican temple, guided by 16th-century ethnohistoric accounts (see Marcus 1978; Nicholson 1971: 438). According to these descriptions, the Mesoamerican temple was generally a rectangular structure with a single opening entering into one of its long sides. Temple structures normally were elevated on truncated pyramid mounds. Most frequently, they were composed of at least two rooms, an outer chamber and a slightly raised, inner, more sacred sanctuary.

As early as 1913, Herbert Spinden (99), writing about the Maya, suggested that a simple room with a door in the center of one of its long sides, was the starting-point for the temple (as well as for Maya palaces) and that this simple room was modified by interior partitions until there was a clear development of the sanctuary or inner sacred chamber. More recently, Joyce Marcus (1983: 230–31) has observed that this basic temple plan is remarkably standard across Mesoamerica, with two-room temples known from major Classic period cities in the Peten (Tikal), the Valley of Oaxaca (Monte Alban), and Central Mexico (Teotihuacan). At Monte Alban, Jorge Acosta (1965) noted that Classic period temples had the same basic plan as those from 200 B.C., and Marcus (1983) and Flannery (1983: 132) have described comparable temple layouts at secondary centers in the Valley of Oaxaca from both epochs. Marcus (1978: 174) also has traced the two-room temple to 16th-century Oaxaca where, as with earlier Oaxacan temples, they generally were positioned in elevated locations. Based on her reading of ethnohistoric accounts, Marcus (1978: 174–75) found that worshippers could enter only the outer room of the temple, while the slightly raised, more sacred, inner chamber was restricted to priests.

Maya temples, at times composed of one or three rooms rather than the more common two, were in general somewhat less homogeneous than those in the Valley of Oaxaca (Pollock 1965; Andrews 1975; Marcus 1978, 1983). Yet as in Oaxaca, these rectangular Maya temple structures (containing relatively little interior space and a single entryway) were normally elevated on pyramidal substructures or platforms. Harry Pollock (1965: 409–11) has described Maya temples as intermediate compared to shrines and palaces in size and elaboration, as well as more regular in form than the latter.

In Central Mexico, the dual sanctuary plan, found at the Templo Mayor, may extend back roughly 1500 years to Teotihuacan (Millon 1976: 238). At the Templo Mayor, each sanctuary had a single room with altars along the back wall, a plan basically similar to one-room temples elsewhere in Mesoamerica (Matos Moctezuma 1982). During Aztec times, a twin temple was also built at Tenayuca in the State of Mexico (Marquina 1951: 164–80). As noted previously by Marcus (1983: 232), the earliest sanctuaries at Tenayuca had only one room with a small altar along the rear wall. Yet following several rebuilding episodes, two standard two-room temples were constructed. Although we do not understand the meaning of the Central Mexican dual temple plan as compared to the single temples found in the Maya region and the State of Oaxaca, it would seem significant that the basic sanctuary plan was followed in each region (Nicholson 1971: 438).

Evolution of the Temple

Although truncated pyramids and more generalized ceremonial structures (e.g., Flannery and Marcus 1983) are almost as old as sedentary farming villages in Mesoamerica, the earliest definitive masonry temples were not constructed until the last centuries B.C. In the Valley of Oaxaca, sequentially rebuilt rectangular two-room temples dated to Monte Alban II (200 B.C.–A.D. 200) have been found on Mound X (just off the centrally-situated Main Plaza) at Monte Alban (Caso 1935; Flannery and Marcus 1983: 82; Flannery 1983: 104) and atop Mound I at the secondary center, San Jose Mogote (Flannery and Marcus 1983: 111–12). In the Maya lowlands at Uaxactun, stone masonry two-chambered temples have been dated to the Tzakol phase (A.D. 250–500); however, perishable temple structures on platforms may have been constructed several centuries earlier (Marcus 1978: 183–84). While the evolutionary history of Central Mexican monumental building is generally less well known, Classic period Teotihuacan temples have a plan basically similar to those in the Peten and the Valley of Oaxaca. As at Maya Uaxactun where the Ricketsons (Ricketson and Ricketson 1937) found a Preclassic era pole-and-thatch dwelling constructed around an altar atop a platform, Cummings (1933) found a Preclassic altar on one of the large oval mounds at Cuicuilco in the Basin of Mexico. Thus, temples built of perishable materials, possibly contemporaneous with the Monte Alban II masonry buildings, may have been constructed in each region.

Thus, as Spinden (1913) and Marcus (1983: 232) have suggested previously, the more formal masonry two-room temple may have evolved from less elaborate structures made from perishable materials. For the Valley of Oaxaca, Flannery and Marcus (1983: 82) see the development of the stereotyped temple plan as a possible indicator of the process of linearization, the usurpation of certain household tasks (rituals) by a central religious authority. They note that the handmade clay figurines, found in earlier houses and possibly used to create ritual scenes, disappear from the archaeological record by Monte Alban II. Certainly, similar processes may have been associated with the development of formal temples at Teotihuacan and in the Early Classic Peten. Thus the development of the temple seems to have been correlated with the rise of an increasingly urbanized, internally differentiated, hierarchical social system in each region. The importance of the latter relationship is supported indirectly by 16th-century ethnohistoric accounts, which document the frequent use of rather modest houses and huts for ritual in the Northern Yucatan, where the polities were less hierarchical at Contact (Tozzer 1941: 152–53). A further intriguing clue to the modest origin of this Mesoamerican institution comes from an analysis of the indigenous words for 'temple'. In Nahuatl (*teocalli*, Dibble and Anderson 1963: 269; Vaillant 1966: 144), Zapotec (*yohopee*, Marcus 1978: 174), Mixtec (*huahi nuhu*, Marcus 1983: 346), and Maya (*kuna*, Tozzer 1921: 299; Marcus 1978: 181), the word for 'temple' can be derived by affixing either 'divine', 'life spirit', or 'sacred' to the word for 'house'.

The Temple As Symbol

Eduardo Matos Moctezuma (1984b) has suggested that the Templo Mayor was the place where the power of the Mexica was actually or symbolically established. He interprets the twin temples of Tlaloc (the god of water and rain) and Huitzilopochtli (the patron deity of the Mexica, the solar god, the war deity) as an ideological reflection of Tenochtitlan's economic foundation, based on agriculture and war tribute. Consequently, for Matos Moctezuma (1984b: 135), "the whole archaeological context associated with the Templo Mayor (offerings, sculptures, rituals, etc.) in some way indicates the economic-religious-political control Tenochtitlan had over its own people and other groups." Furthermore, the Great Temple and its associated rituals are interpreted as inseparably integrated with and a reflection of the myth of the god's Huitzilopochtli's birth, an account in which the patron deity is born fully armed from his mother's (Coatlicue) womb and rises to do battle with his siblings (Matos Moctezuma 1984b: 135–36).

Although Matos Moctezuma has not substantiated all the specific details of his model, there do seem to be sufficient evidential threads to imply that pre-Hispanic temples were symbolic of the communities, people, or elite who built and occupied them. In the Mixteca Alta, Postclassic period place-signs incorporated depictions of seemingly specific temples in the identifying glyphs that are thought to name particular towns (Smith 1973: 246). During the later (Classic and Postclassic periods) history of pre-Columbian Mesoamerica, the great regional centers (Teotihuacan, Tikal, Monte Alban, Tula, Tenochtitlan) generally contained many more and larger temples than lesser sites. Archetypically, no Mesoamerican city ever dwarfed the settlements in its regional hinterland to a greater degree than Classic era Teotihuacan (more than 100,000 people estimated), and the site also had more religious structures than any other Middle American center (Millon 1973; Marcus 1983: 222). Not only did each of the more than 2,000 multi-family apartment compounds (housing an estimated 60–100 people) have at least one temple, but 100 religious structures were constructed along the city's central "Street of the Dead" (Millon 1976, 1981). The great sanctity of Teotihuacan and its main street also is implied by the use of the Tablero-talud facade (the architectural symbol for temples at Teotihuacan) on virtually all platforms, including residential compounds and administrative structures, for roughly two continuous kilometers along the "Street of the Dead" (Millon 1981: 228–29).

The argument for the temple as a symbolic representation of place is perhaps even more convincingly supported by the pattern of destruction and depopulation at Teotihuacan. The city was never abandoned or destroyed completely, and evidence for combat and bloodshed are lacking. Yet during the 7th and 8th centuries A.D., the decline of the great center was marked by the systematic burning of the monumental architecture along the "Street of the Dead," as well as by the selected destruction of other temples and public buildings across the site. While most of the city remained intact, civic and ceremonial structures were deliberately set on fire and ritually destroyed. The most concentrated damage was directed at the sanctified center of the city (Millon 1981: 235–38). Furthermore, Millon (1981: 238; see also Adams 1966: 148–49) notes that the ritual destruction of monumental symbols and structures was a recurrent process in ancient Mesoamerica, associated across time and space with the demise of great centers.

Although the importance of pre-Hispanic Mesoamerican communities seems well correlated with the size and grandeur of their temples, the mechanism for this relationship is understood imperfectly. Clearly, the amount of labor that could have been called on and organized must have been one significant factor. For example, when the Templo Mayor was reconstructed during the reign of Moctezuma Ilhuicamina (A.D. 1440–1453), workers from newly conquered city-states under Aztec control were recruited to do the job (Carrasco 1982: 186). Tozzer (1941: 151–52) has suggested that these periodic renovations and rebuildings, seen in the archaeological record of ceremonial structures, may pertain to the purification rituals conducted at the end of the 52 year cycle. Yet the eleven rebuildings of the Templo Mayor, completed over less than two centuries (Matos Moctezuma 1984a), indicate that in at least certain cases renovations and expansions were enacted more often than every 52 years. Prosperity and conquest may have prompted and been symbolized by the rapid growth and elaboration of the Great Temple of Aztec Tenochtitlan.

The Priesthood and the Activities of the Temple

Documentary accounts of temples, priests, and their activities, recounted during the Contact period by European clerics and conquistadors, still provide the most detailed information on pre-Columbian religion in Mesoamerica. Yet in recent decades, these findings have been supplemented through archaeological research, as well as by significant new interpretations of ancient Mesoamerican ritual that have been drawn largely from recent analyses of Classic period Maya art, iconography, and inscriptions. These breakthroughs have yielded additional support for the belief that blood, and hence various kinds of sacrifice (often though not exclusively conducted in the temple), was central to many Mesoamerican religions, and not merely to the Aztecs, as has been known from 16th-century accounts. This discussion first reviews the late pre-Hispanic historical materials and then gradually moves to a consideration of relevant archaeological data.

Several recurrent themes concerning the priesthood and temple organization can be drawn from contemporary syntheses of late pre-Hispanic religion in Central Mexico (Nicholson 1971; Berdan 1982; Carrasco 1982), the Maya region (Tozzer 1941; Roys 1943; Thompson 1970; Marcus 1978), and the Valley of Oaxaca (Spores 1965; Marcus 1978; Flannery and Marcus 1983). In each area, temples were associated with a priesthood that was hierarchically structured and internally specialized (Thompson 1970: 167–70; Carrasco 1971: 358; Marcus 1978: 174, 181). The highest priestly positions were full-time, and years of training generally were required to reach that status. Young children, frequently from high-status families, were recruited into the priesthood (e.g., Marcus 1978: 175), with advancement through the priestly hierarchy based on a variety of factors (including birthright, training, and devotion).

Mesoamerican priests, as described at Contact, were involved with a suite of generally similar activities that crosscut both political and ethnic divisions. In addition to their close involvement with ceremonies and rituals, they had important roles in the education of the young, divination, ancestor worship, and the keeping of the ritual calendar. Aztec and Postclassic Maya priests also tended anthropomorphized "idols" of deities (made of wood and stone) inside their temples, and 16th-century Spanish accounts describe a similar practice among the Contact-era Zapotec priests of Oaxaca (see Spores 1965: 970). However, Marcus (1978: 174) has argued that 16th-century Spanish clerics, swayed by their classical education and knowledge of the Greco-Roman pantheon, misunderstood Zapotec religion, misconceiving Oaxacan ancestor worship for "idolatrous" behaviors honoring a pantheon of anthropomorphized deities. Marcus (1978: 180) also suggests that the Classic period Maya were not image worshippers, and that it was the Nahua speakers of Central Mexico who introduced idolatry to the Yucatan Maya during the later Postclassic period (see also Roys 1943: 72; Thompson 1970: 187; Morley, Brainerd, and Sharer 1983: 461-62).

Most scholars agree that ceremonial and civic activities were very closely intertwined in ancient Mesoamerica. As Berdan (1982: 130) has suggested, perhaps this distinction was not even made in the Mesoamerican world. At Conquest in Central Mexican Cholula, the two ruling offices were filled by priests from the cult of the town's patron god, Quetzalcoatl (Carrasco 1971: 372). In Aztec society, the children of nobles were educated by priests (Carrasco 1971: 356). In addition, Aztec rulers took a very active role in rituals and ceremonies, and various rituals (including sacrifices) were associated with political events such as coronations (e.g., Berdan 1982: 132). Priestly divinations were used to select the appropriate days for important political events (Hodge 1984: 22). Senior and "retired" priests also were given very important advisory roles in the councils of Aztec rulers (Carrasco 1971).

For the 16th-century Yucatan, Landa recorded the close association between high priests and lords; the priests used their knowledge to give advice to (and foretell the future for) political rulers (Tozzer 1941: 27). The second sons of lords were educated by priests (Tozzer 1941: 27). Regarding the Contact period Zapotecs, Flannery and Marcus (1983: 82) note: "church and state were united to the extent that priests were recruited from the sons of nobility, and the Zapotec lord himself underwent a year of religious training before he took office. After all, his royal ancestors were semi-divine interceders between his community and the great supernatural forces whose favor the Zapotec sought to incur."

Although the variety of calendric and non-calendric activities and festivals was enormously diverse across Mesoamerica, there was a series of activities and themes that permeated 16th-century Mesoamerican ritual performance. Significantly, these key ideological behaviors also seem to have had a long history in religious practice. As cited in the previous paragraph, communication with revered ancestors, spirits, and gods was central to the ritual activities of Mesoamerican priests (see also Tozzer 1941: 129-31; Nicholson 1971: 409; Marcus 1978: 175, 182-83). A key mechanism for these contacts was through offerings and sacrifice.

The centrality of offerings and sacrifice to Aztec ritual and ceremony has long been known (if not always completely understood). In his overview of Central Mexican religion, Nicholson (1971: 431-32) noted that "nearly every ceremony featured offerings" with the most common gifts for the sacred including food, flowers, rubber-spattered papers, clothing, and incense. Important Aztec rituals normally included some kind of death sacrifice. Even though the execution of animals, particularly birds, was most common, scholars have recognized the Aztec custom of human sacrifice as having been practiced at a magnitude not approached by other Mesoamerican peoples (Nicholson 1971: 432; Anawalt 1982; Conrad and Demarest 1984; Ingham 1984).

Based on 16th-century accounts, scholars have known that the elite of Tenochtitlan considered themselves to be the children of the sun or chosen people, responsible for keeping the cosmos in order. They believed that the continued existence of the sun and the earth only could be achieved by offering the deities a regular diet of blood and hearts (Anawalt 1982). Although Aztec sacrificial rites were by no means uniform, the rituals generally were enacted in or near the temple with certain classes of priests charged with dispatching the victims (frequently, though not always, prisoners). To the Aztec, blood was "precious water" (Ingham 1984: 391), and ritual self-immolation also was an important aspect of offerings and penitence (Nicholson 1971: 433). Priests were the usual practitioners of auto-sacrifice, drawing their blood from ear lobes, tongues, legs, or genitals with maguey spines or blades made from obsidian, and then offering it to the gods.

Although Aztec human sacrifice, particularly during the last century before Contact, was carried out at a scale probably never seen before in the Mesoamerican world (Berdan 1982: 116), the basis for this sacrificial tradition, including blood offerings, the ritual importance of blood, and self-immolation, are understood now to be much deeper in time and more widespread in space (Anawalt 1982: 42). Human sacrifice and bloodletting implements have an apparently much longer history in Mesoamerica than the masonry temple (Flannery and Marcus 1976; Flannery, Marcus, and Kowalewski 1981; MacNeish 1981). As with 16th-century Aztec priests, principal duties of late pre-Conquest priests in Oaxaca and Yucatan included temple sacrifices of animals and humans, the self-extraction of blood, and the offering of blood to supernatural elements (Tozzer 1941; Roys 1943: 80–82; Marcus 1978: 175, 182). Sacrifice also was a recurrent event in surviving pre-Hispanic codices (bark paper or animal skin books), including pictorial documents not written by the Aztec.

Bloodletting and, to a lesser degree, human sacrifice were significant themes in the carved stone stelae, temple murals, cave paintings, and polychrome pottery of the Classic Maya (A.D. 300–900) (Joralemon

1974; Marcus 1978: 185–86; Schele 1984; Stone 1985). In Classic Maya stelae, lords or priests as well as their consorts frequently were depicted holding bloodletters and taking their blood, while on other monuments women are shown holding vessels of blood-spattered paper (e.g., Proskouriakoff 1960). Insight into this entire Mesoamerican tradition perhaps can be gleaned from Maya languages, where a linguistic relationship has been noted between the word for bloodletting and that for the nurturing or breast feeding of a child by its parent (Schele 1984: 33; Stone 1985: 25). Thus, as a mother's milk provides sustenance to a child, a bloodletter could have nurtured the supernatural world, maintaining the earth's natural order and fertility. Blood rituals can be seen as sacrificial practices that affirmed and established the unequal access to power and status in Mesoamerican societies (Marcus 1978; Conrad and Demarest 1984), while blood-producers (e.g., bloodletters, captive takers, sacrificial priests) were positioned as the insurers or sustainers of a people's or a community's well-being (Schele 1984).

Archaeological excavations of Mesoamerican temples have supported and confirmed the historical accounts of key temple functions and activities. Matos Moctezuma's (1984a: 83) Templo Mayor excavations revealed a slab of black volcanic rock in front of the sanctuary of Huitzilopochtli. The stone's dimensions and placement conform with those described for a sacrificial altar by the 16th-century Spanish. Decapitated skulls (though no complete bodies) and large, often decorated stone knives also have been found in quantity during the excavations. At Late Postclassic Mayapan, a key Maya site in Northern Yucatan, most of the large chert and flint, "sacrificial" knives uncovered were associated with the site's ceremonial precincts (Pollock et al. 1962: fig. 28). Many remains of burned copal incense also were found on temple floors (Pollock et al. 1982: 404–5). Circular burned areas on the floor of a Monte Alban II Oaxacan temple at San Jose Mogote suggest that incense burners were lit there as well (Marcus 1983: 222). Inner rooms of San Jose Mogote temples also yielded ripple-flaked "sacrificial" obsidian knives, as well as dozens of razor-sharp obsidian blades that likely were employed in bloodletting rituals (Marcus 1983: 222).

Economics and the Temple

In his paper, Winston Davis mentions that through history great market and trade centers in Japan often were associated with important temples and shrines. Thomas Lee (1978: 2) has noted that this interdependence also held in ancient Mesoamerica, where there was a frequent spatial correspondence between important religious sanctuaries (pilgrimage destinations) and trading ports, including Mayan Xicalango, Chetumal, and Cozumel (Chapman 1959; Sabloff and Rathje 1975). Other key civic-ceremonial cities in highland Mesoamerica (e.g., Teotihuacan, Tula, Tenochtitlan-Tlatelolco, Mitla) also were known as very important locations for production and exchange. In addition, many of the early Spanish chroniclers (Duran 1971: 275) described the close proximity between the plaza or marketplace and the temple precinct in late pre-Hispanic centers (Lee 1978: 2).

At Contact, the temples of the Aztec Triple Alliance (Tenochtitlan, Texcoco, and Tlacopan) received tribute from surrounding towns. Recurring levies were used to fund special ceremonial events, while lands were yielded to provide daily sustenance (Berdan 1982: 40). Symbolic tributary offerings, including shells, swordfish, crocodiles, gems, and an array of other goods exotic to Central Mexico also were incorporated into each stage of construction fill at the Templo Mayor in at least 90 dedicatory caches. David Carrasco (1982: 182–83) has suggested that these items, 80% of which came from distant provinces under the dominion of the Aztec empire, served to sanctify those conquests and the expansion of the Aztec tribute domain. Yet unlike Aztec temples, the 16th-century Yucatan Maya temples did not receive specified allotments of tribute (Roys 1943: 80), and formal temple extractions also were not significant in other parts of the Mesoamerican world. Although Berdan (1982: 40) has noted that produce was stored periodically in and near 16th-century Central Mexican temples, there is no evidence to suggest that any pre-Columbian Mesoamerican temples engaged in the storage or redistribution of goods at or near the scale practiced by certain temples in the ancient Old World.

Despite the spatial co-occurrence of key trade and religious activities in important Mesoamerican cites, there is relatively little to suggest that the pre-Hispanic temple was involved directly in commodity production. An exception is within and adjacent to the Temple of the Moon complex at Teotihuacan, where the production of obsidian blades, cores, and bifaces was carried out (Millon 1981: 224; Spence 1981). This seemingly aberrant case makes more sense if we consider 16th-century documents which describe ritual bloodletting as one of the principal uses for obsidian (Marcus 1983: 223 has commented that auto-sacrifice would be one activity for which obsidian would be superior to flint). As obsidian worked at Teotihuacan was exchanged great distances, tools produced under the auspices of one of the largest temples in this sacred city may have been used in ritual bloodletting across Mesoamerica (Marcus 1983: 223).

A general comparison of the Mesoamerican bark paper codices and the Near Eastern temple tablets provides a final indicator of the comparatively lesser economic role played by the temple in

Mesoamerica compared with religious institutions in the ancient Old World. Whereas the majority of the former, written by Mesoamerican priests, pertain to divination, sacred knowledge, astronomy, and ritual, many of the latter detail economic transactions.

Conclusion

Although the direct economic role of the temple does not seem to have been great, religion (including the temple) was critically important in the Mesoamerican world as a mechanism of social cohesion, control, integration, and communication. So many key Mesoamerican ideological conceptions (e.g., the 260-day ritual calendar, the feathered serpent, supernaturals associated with rain and lightning, blood sacrifice, and the basic temple layout) were widespread in space and time that these symbols must have been shared broadly and of great significance. Temple ritual and religion clearly was an important means for binding Mesoamerica's ethnically and linguistically diverse peoples both within and across polity boundaries (Nicholson 1971: 433–34).

The Mesoamerican world lacked wheeled transport, beasts of burden, major road systems, as well as metal implements and weapons (although metal ornaments were made), yet towns of 10,000 were commonplace, and cities larger than 100,000 people were built more than once. A tributary domain, constructed by the Aztec, stretched from Central Mexico to Guatemala, and another large, hierarchically interconnected network was centered at earlier Teotihuacan. Mesoamerican polities generally were organized hierarchically, and diverse economies were integrated despite transportation limitations. Impressive architectural construction programs, requiring enormous labor forces, were implemented. How else, but through the development of powerful and highly sophisticated systems of religion and statecraft, can we account for the maintenance and survival of these large, complex Mesoamerican cities and polities, for hundreds and perhaps even thousands of years?

Reference List

Acosta, Jorge R.
  1965   Preclassic and Classic Architecture of Oaxaca. Pp. 814–36 in *Handbook of Middle American Indians*, vol. 3, ed. G. R. Willey. Austin: University of Texas.

Adams, Robert McC.
  1966   *The Evolution of Urban Society.* Chicago: Aldine-Atherton.

Anawalt, Patricia R.
1982 Understanding Aztec Human Sacrifice. *Archaeology* 35: 38–45.

Andrews, George F.
1975 *Maya Cities: Placemaking and Urbanization.* Norman: University of Oklahoma.

Berdan, Frances F.
1982 *The Aztecs of Central Mexico: An Imperial Society.* New York: Holt, Rinehart, and Winston.

Blanton, Richard E., and Gary Feinman
1984 The Mesoamerican World System. *American Anthropologist* 86: 673–82.

Blanton, Richard E. et al.
1981 *Ancient Mesoamerica: A Comparison of Change in Three Regions.* Cambridge: Cambridge University.

Carrasco, David
1982 *Quetzalcoatl and the Irony of Empire.* Chicago: University of Chicago.

Carrasco, Pedro
1971 Social Organization of Ancient Mexico. Pp. 349–75 in *Handbook of Middle American Indians,* vol. 10, ed. G. F. Ekholm and I. Bernal. Austin: University of Texas.

Caso, Alfonso
1935 *Las exploraciones en Monte Albán, temperada 1934–1935.* Instituto Panamericano de Geografia e Historia, Publicacion 18. Mexico: Tacubaya.

Chapman, Anne M.
1959 *Puertos de Intercambio en Mesoamérica Prehispánica.* Instituto Nacional de Antropología e Historia, Serie de Historia. Mexico: Instituto Nacional de Antropología e Historia.

Conrad, Geoffrey W., and Arthur A. Demarest
1984 *Religion and Empire: The Dynamics of Aztec and Inca Expansionism.* Cambridge: Cambridge University.

Cummings, Byron C.
1933 Cuicuilco and the Archaic Culture of Mexico. *University of Arizona Social Science Bulletin* 4: 1–56.

Dibble, Charles E., and Arthur J. O. Anderson
1963 *Florentine Codex, General History of the Things of New Spain (Fray Bernardino de Sahagun), Book 11-Earthly Things.* Santa Fe: School of American Research and University of Utah.

Duran, Fray Diego
1971 *Book of the Gods and Rites and the Ancient Calendar,* tr. and ed. F. Horcasitas and D. Heyden. Norman: University of Oklahoma.

Flannery, Kent V.
1983   The Legacy of the Early Urban Period: An Ethnohistoric Approach to Monte Alban's Temples, Residences, and Royal Tombs. Pp. 132–36 in *The Cloud People*, ed. K. V. Flannery and J. Marcus. New York: Academic.

Flannery, Kent V., and Joyce Marcus
1976   Evolution of the Public Building in Formative Oaxaca. Pp. 205–21 in *Cultural Change and Continuity: Essays in Honor of James B. Griffin*, ed. C. Cleland. New York: Academic.

Flannery, Kent V., and Joyce Marcus (eds.)
1983   *The Cloud People: Divergent Evolution of the Zapotec and Mixtec Civilizations.* New York: Academic.

Flannery, Kent V.; Joyce Marcus; and Stephen A. Kowalewski
1981   The Preceramic and Formative of the Valley of Oaxaca. Pp. 48–93 in *Supplement to the Handbook of Middle American Indians*, vol. 1, ed. J. A. Sabloff. Austin: University of Texas.

Hodge, Mary G.
1984   *Aztec City-States.* University of Michigan, Museum of Anthropology, Memoir 18. Ann Arbor: University of Michigan.

Ingham, John M.
1984   Human Sacrifice at Tenochtitlan. *Comparative Studies in Society and History* 26: 379–400.

Joralemon, David
1974   Ritual Blood Sacrifice among the Ancient Maya: Part I. Pp. 59–75 in *Primera Mesa Redonda de Palenque, Part II*, ed. M. G. Robertson. Pebble Beach, Calif.: Robert Louis Stevenson School.

Lee, Thomas A., Jr.
1978   Introduction. Pp. 1–4 in *Mesoamerican Communication Routes and Cultural Contacts*, ed. T. A. Lee, Jr., and C. Navarrete. New World Archaeological Foundation, Paper 40. Provo, Utah: Brigham Young University.

MacNeish, Richard S.
1981   Tehuacan's Accomplishments. Pp. 31–47 in *Supplement to the Handbook of Middle American Indians*, vol. 1, ed. J. A. Sabloff. Austin: University of Texas.

Marcus, Joyce
1978   Archaeology and Religion: A Comparison of the Zapotec and Maya. *World Archaeology* 10: 172–91.
1983   On the Nature of the Mesoamerican City. Pp. 195–242 in *Prehistoric Settlement Patterns: Essays in Honor of Gordon R. Willey*, ed. E. Z. Vogt and R. M. Leventhal. Albuquerque: University of New Mexico.

Marquina, Ignacio
1951   *Arquitectura Prehispanica.* Memórias del Instituto Nacional de

Antropología e Historia 1. Mexico: Instituto Nacional de Antropología e Historia.

Matos Moctezuma, Eduardo
1982   *El Templo Mayor de Tenochtitlan: Planos, Cortes, y Perspectivas.*
        Mexico: Instituto Nacional de Antropología e Historia.
1984a   The Great Temple of Tenochtitlan. *Scientific American* 251: 80–89.
1984b   The Templo Mayor of Tenochtitlan: Economics and Ideology.
        Pp. 133–64 in *Ritual Human Sacrifice in Mesoamerica*, ed. E. H.
        Boone. Washington, D.C.: Dumbarton Oaks.

Millon, Rene
1973   *The Teotihuacan Map.* Austin: University of Texas.
1976   Social Relations in Ancient Teotihuacan. Pp. 205–48 in *The Valley
        of Mexico*, ed. E. R. Wolf. Albuquerque: University of New
        Mexico.
1981   Teotihuacan: City, State, and Civilization. Pp. 198–243 in *Supplement
        to the Handbook of Middle American Indians*, vol. 1, ed.
        J. A. Sabloff. Austin: University of Texas.

Morley, Sylvanus G.; George W. Brainerd; and Robert J. Sharer
1983   *The Ancient Maya.* Stanford: Stanford University.

Nicholson, Henry B.
1971   Religion in Pre-Hispanic Central Mexico. Pp. 395–446 in *Handbook
        of Middle American Indians*, vol. 10, ed. G. F. Ekholm and
        I. Bernal. Austin: University of Texas.

Pollock, Harry E. D.
1965   Architecture of the Maya Lowlands. Pp. 378–440 in *Handbook of
        Middle American Indians*, vol. 2, ed. G. R. Willey. Austin: University
        of Texas.

Pollock, Harry E. D. et al.
1962   *Mayapan, Yucatan, Mexico.* Carnegie Institution of Washington publication
        619. Washington, D.C.: Carnegie Institution of Washington.

Proskouriakoff, Tatiana
1960   Historical Implications of a Pattern of Dates at Piedras Negras,
        Guatemala. *American Antiquity* 25: 454–75.

Ricketson, O. G., Jr., and E. B. Ricketson
1937   *Uaxactun, Guatemala, Group E, 1926–1931.* Carnegie Institution of
        Washington publication 477. Washington, D.C.: Carnegie Institution
        of Washington.

Roys, Ralph L.
1943   *The Indian Background of Colonial Yucatan.* Carnegie Institution
        of Washington publication 548. Washington, D.C.: Carnegie Institution
        of Washington.

Sabloff, Jeremy A., and William R. Rathje (eds.)
1975   *A Study of Changing Precolumbian Commercial Systems.* Peabody

Museum Monograph 3. Cambridge, Mass.: Peabody Museum of Anthropology and Ethnology.

Schele, Linda
1984   Human Sacrifice Among the Classic Maya. Pp. 7–48 in *Ritual Human Sacrifice in Mesoamerica*, ed. E. H. Boone. Washington, D.C.: Dumbarton Oaks.

Smith, Mary Elizabeth
1973   *Picture Writing from Ancient Southern Mexico*. Norman: University of Oklahoma.

Spence, Michael W.
1981   Obsidian Production and the State in Teotihuacan. *American Antiquity* 46: 769–88.

Spinden, Herbert J.
1913   *A Study of Maya Art*. Memoirs of the Peabody Museum of American Archaeology and Ethnology 6. Cambridge, Mass.: Peabody Museum.

Spores, Ronald
1965   The Zapotec and Mixtec at Spanish Contact. Pp. 962–87 in *Handbook of Middle American Indians*, vol. 3, ed. G. R. Willey. Austin: University of Texas.

Stone, Andrea
1985   The Moon Goddess at Naj Tunich. *Mexicon* 7: 23–29.

Thompson, J. Eric S.
1970   *Maya History and Religion*. Norman: University of Oklahoma.

Tozzer, Alfred M.
1921   *A Maya Grammar with Bibliography and Appraisement of the Works Noted*. Peabody Museum of Archaeology and Ethnology Papers, 9. Cambridge, Mass.: Peabody Museum.
1941   *Landa's Relacion de las Cosas de Yucatan*. Peabody Museum of American Archaeology and Ethnology Papers, 18. Cambridge, Mass.: Peabody Museum.

Vaillant, George C.
1966   *Aztecs of Mexico*. Middlesex, England: Penguin.

Wallerstein, Immanuel
1974   *The Modern World System: Capitalist Agriculture and the Origins of the European World-Economy in the Sixteenth Century*. New York: Academic.

Temples and Shrines in Japan: Their Social Functions

Winston Davis

In a collection of papers dealing with the role of temples in society, it may seem odd to introduce the word shrine. Yet, if we are to understand the temple in Japanese society, this is necessary. Japanese religion is thoroughly syncretistic. Its main ingredient is Shinto, itself a syncretistic blend of several prehistoric traditions including magic, animism and shamanism. Shinto practices and values seem to give a special Japanese "flavor" to the various schools and sects of Buddhism, Taoism, Confucianism, and Christianity which were introduced in later history.

In prehistoric times, worship might take place before a mysteriously shaped rock, a mountain perfectly formed in the shape of a cone, or a waterfall thought to be the abode of a god or spirit. A rope (today called a *shimenawa*) might be strung up to mark off the site as sacred space, but generally a permanent building was not used. Perhaps the concept of deity was too fleeting to merit a permanent place of worship (cf. Usener's *Augenblicksgötter*).[1] Or the mobility of the primitive hunters and gatherers of this period may have discouraged the use of permanent buildings for religious rites. It was probably during the Yayoi Period (ca. 250 b.c. to ca. a.d. 250) that permanent places of worship first appeared. Originally modeled after the rice granaries introduced during this period, their general outlines can still be seen in the Grand Shrines of Ise.[2]

With the coming of Buddhism in the sixth century, the Japanese gave their indigenous religious practices a new name—"Shinto," the Way of the Kami—to set them apart from the worship of the Buddha. They also used special words to distinguish the Shinto place of worship from the Buddhist temple. Today, the Buddhist temple is known generically as the *otera*; the Shinto shrine as the *jinja, omiya,* or *jingū*.

---

1. Such deities can still be found in Japan today. See for example the *hayari-gami* described in my essay "Pilgrimage and World Renewal: A Study of Religion and Social Values in Tokugawa Japan, Part II," *History of Religions* 23 (1984) 215.

2. Throughout the centuries, the primitive architecture of Ise's wooden fanes has been preserved by a curious custom. The shrines have been built and then deliberately torn down and rebuilt in the same way every twenty years since about the middle of the first millennium a.d.

While Shinto-Buddhist syncretism has affected even the form of buildings, these terms generally denote distinctive architectural styles. The
Shinto shrine is really a house for the kami. Worshipers do not enter
the shrine, but rather stand before it, clap their hands and make their
prayer. A Buddhist temple, on the other hand, is built to house or
enclose a congregation of worshipers. When they are busy, or do not
wish to enter the temple, people simply stand in front of the temple
and offer up a brief prayer to the Buddha. In this case, etiquette calls
for the worshiper to fold his hands in prayer (*gasshō*). But, in fact,
most Japanese forget this and clap their hands as though worshiping
the Shinto kami.

In this paper, I shall not be concerned about the temple or shrine
buildings as such. Nor am I interested in the words the Japanese have
used for them. Rather, I shall concentrate on the social roles of
temples and shrines as *institutionalized places of worship*. Now, if we
think of temples and shrines as places of *worship* we must understand
what worship means in the context of Japanese religious life. I shall
argue that while temples and shrines have played a wide variety of
functions in Japanese history, since archaic times their basic function
has been to serve as a place where *magical and ritual exchanges can
take place* between human beings, on the one hand, and the kami,
buddhas, and ancestral spirits, on the other. This exchange is basically
similar to that which took place in temples throughout the ancient
world. It was given classical expression in the Latin phrase *do ut
des*—roughly: "I am giving this gift to you, god, so that you will give
me . . ."—and by the Sanskrit equivalent, *dadami se, dehi me*.[3] Looked
at in this way, the temple or shrine is a permanent "stock exchange"
or spiritual-material "market place" where gifts are presented to the
divine powers in order to secure magical boons of health, wealth, and
security. They are also places where people offer gifts and sacrifices
for boons they have already received. I regard this exchange as basic
insofar as it is hard to imagine anything else going on in temples and
shrines if these "transactions" were to come to an end. Later in
history, sacrifice might be "spiritualized" and become a "sacrifice of
praise and thanksgiving" as the *Book of Common Prayer* has it, but
the temple and/or shrine seems to retain its archaic function as the
permanent institution for conducting ritual exchanges between mortals
and immortals.

At this point, some may object that my concept of the temple
contradicts the Buddhist denial of the kind of personal deities who are

---

3. Marcel Mauss, *The Gift: Forms and Functions of Exchange in Archaic Societies*
(trans. Ian Cunnison; London: Cohen and West, 1969) 12–15.

believed to enter into such exchange relations. Furthermore, my definition seems to leave no room for meditation, for the meditator is not "using" meditation in order to secure magical boons—at least, he is not supposed to! The great Zen master, Dōgen Zenji (1200–1253), was especially critical of those who tried to use meditation for any extrinsic end, even the attainment of nirvana itself. All of these objections are valid. There is indeed a great tension between the spirit of classical Buddhism (and Zen, for that matter) and the actual practices of Buddhist temples. That is why some Zen practitioners, such as Professor Abe Masao, draw a distinction between the "Zen of the temples" and Zen itself. Since I am dealing with the social functions of temples and shrines, I must concentrate on what the Japanese people *actually do* when they "worship" the kami and the buddhas. What is "Tanaka san" doing when, on his way to work, he pauses before the tutelary deity of his neighborhood, claps his hands, and prays? What is he doing when he participates in the Shinto festival of the same shrine, raucously shouldering the divine palinquin with his (male) neighbors, making his way through the streets of the town— perhaps slightly inebriated—to the rhythmic chant "*wasshoi, wasshoi, wasshoi?*" What is the same Tanaka san doing when, in a more somber mood, he attends a memorial service for one of his ancestors in his family's Buddhist temple? These are the things that shall concern us, not the (unfortunately) rare practice of *zazen* (Zen meditation), or the refined speculations of the Buddhist philosopher.

The Many Functions of Temples and Shrines

In Japan, just as in other countries, religious institutions have played a wide variety of complex roles. In the past, temples have functioned not only as religious centers, but as secular institutions. Some, for example, became powerful landlords equipped with their own warrior-monks (*sōhei*). Like the Cistercian abbeys of Europe, Japanese temples and shrines have even served as banks.[4] In spite of monastic rules to the contrary, they have engaged in the cultivation of the land, the lending of money, and the brewing of intoxicating drink.

---

4. As early as A.D. 620, Chinese Buddhists were setting up temple banks called "Inexhaustible Treasuries," perhaps in response to the "donation bank" mentioned by the Vimalakirti Sutra. The "Third Period" sect was especially active in the creation of these banks. Money from the banks was used to repair temples and to help the poor and the sick. It is believed that these early banks influenced the later Chinese and Japanese Buddhist credit unions and mutual financing societies. See Richard H. Robinson and Willard L. Johnson, *The Buddhist Religion: A Historical Introduction* (Belmont: Wadsworth, 1982) 175–76.

Among their latent functions, one of the most important has been the legitimation of power. From the Grand Shrine of Ise (the shrine of the imperial family) to the smallest village fane, temples and shrines have been symbols of authority. The earliest Japanese emperors and empresses were both political and shamanistic figures. Even in the twentieth century the emperor continues to function as the high priest of Shinto. The ancient word for government (*matsuri-goto*) was essentially the same as the word used for religious festivals today (*omatsuri*). In Japanese villages, where headmen double as Shinto priests, shrines function to legitimate local authority.

Shinto has many faces. In the sanctuaries of the court, its rites are directed toward the well-being of the country itself and the sanctification of power. However, in folk Shinto, sectarian Shinto, and the Shinto-based New Religions the function of the shrine is often patently magical. It performs many of its social functions through annual festivals. Through the lustrations of the festival the community is purified; through the excitement of its athletic contests and the parade of its palanquin or god-cart (*omikoshi*) the community is ritually renewed; through the prayers of its priest, prosperity and peace are ensured for still another year. The shrine also provides magical services on a more routine, daily basis. Visitors to the shrine are often seen tossing stones at the shrine gate (*torii*). If the stone lands on the top of the gate and stays there, they will be lucky. Another example comes from the Kitano Shrine in Kyoto. Carved into the base of a stone lantern standing in front of the shrine is a small bas-relief of Daikoku, one of Japan's Seven Gods of Luck. One often sees people lined up before the lantern trying to put small pebbles in the hollow eye sockets of the image. Behind this curious custom seems to be the simple idea that if someone gives Daikoku eyes, the god, in turn, will be obliged to make that person lucky.[5]

While the Shinto parish is the embodiment of the entire local community, the Buddhist temple is generally associated with the family. The priest acts as the "psychopomp" for the souls of the dead whose mortal remains rest in the graveyard attached to the temple. The temple's primary function has been to secure the repose of the family's ancestors, and thereby the good fortune of the living. From earliest times, Buddhist temples have also functioned as schools. Today, they often operate pre-schools and day-care centers for the

---

5. In this case, magic seems to invert the usual exchange relationship between gods and worshipers. Usually, the deity is the benefactor and therefore holds the upper hand. Here, the god is put under an obligation by receiving a benefit from his worshipers. Magical relationships of this sort seem to give the individual a (somewhat shaky) handle on fate.

children of working mothers. (Recently, these schools have become an important source of temple revenues.)

Buddhist temples are also festival centers. Like the Shinto *omatsuri*, the Buddhist festival is intended for the rejuvenation of the community and for bringing it good fortune. At the *Obon*, the All Souls Festival held in midsummer, families come to the temple to entertain the spirits of their ancestors. In Tochigi, Miyagi and Ibaraki prefectures, the Obon dances (*bon-odori*) are actually called Good Harvest Dances (*hōnen-odori*) and are performed not just as entertainment for the ancestral spirits but as prayers for a bumper crop. *Setsubun*, held in early February to celebrate the beginning of spring, is an even better example of a Buddhist festival of good luck. Many temples invite a "Man of the Year" (*toshi-otoko*)—usually a famous actor, wrestler, or entertainer—to throw beans over the heads of the crowds which gather in the courtyard of the temple. Chanting "out with demons, in with good luck!" (*oni wa soto, fuku wa uchi*), the Man of the Year brings good luck to himself and to those who are able to catch the beans.[6]

Religious systems have a variety of functions. But each system does not necessarily stress the same functions. Indeed, this is what makes the comparative study of religion interesting and important. Each tradition tends to sanctify, specialize in, or dilate upon certain segments of the subconscious, a definite range of emotions, a typical way of doing things, a certain arrangement of priorities, a definitive set of normative attitudes towards other people and towards the nature and purpose of its own rituals and magic. As Weberians (like Clifford Geertz) might put it, each tradition has its own "ethos." While temples and shrines have played a wide variety of roles in Japanese society, in this paper I will concentrate primarily on what I see as their most basic function: the purveying, securing or enhancing of good luck.[7] Crass as this may be, it seems to me to be the primary goal of worship in popular Japanese religious life. Like their Far East Asian neighbors, the Japanese seem to be obsessed with good luck. They have lucky and unlucky days, animals, directions, numbers,

---

6. In one case, however, Buddhism is not connected with good luck, but its opposite. There is a popular superstition that if the first person one meets in the morning is a priest, the whole day will be unlucky. (In contrast to this, if a bird dropping falls on a person's head, it is thought to portend good luck!)

7. In this paper, when I refer to the purveying, securing or enhancing of "good luck," I have in mind the improvement of material circumstances and life chances by trans-empirical (i.e., religious or magical) means. I will use "luck" as a technical term, applying it both to religions based on karma (where every effect has a cause) and to religions of providence and grace (which depend upon divine will).

words, names, and years of age (*yakudoshi*).[8] They worship auspicious gods and spirits and try to stay on the right side of inauspicious
ones. This magical ethos seems to dominate all of the popular religious
traditions of Asia.[9] In Japan, magic is purveyed to the community at
large by the Shinto parish, to the family and the dead by Buddhist
family temples, and to the individual by prayer-temples, pilgrimage
sites, and religious institutions in general.

The central role of magic in religions which are as close to the
soil as Japan's popular religions are should come as no revelation.
Weber pointed out, "social strata that are dependent upon agricultural
production tend toward magic or religious indifference."[10] Indeed, a
combination of magic and secularism is exactly what one finds in
Japan today. In most cases, popular Japanese religion can be regarded as "slow magic," its magic "fast religion."[11] Thus, "considered
from the unbiased vantage point of statistical significance, Japan's
Great Tradition virtually *is* her Little Tradition."[12] When people have
no need for magical assistance, many become openly indifferent to
religion. Statistics indicate that about 70% of the present-day population fall into this category.[13]

Since I have discussed the magical functions of Shinto and Shinto-
based New Religions elsewhere, I will confine my initial remarks to
Buddhism.[14] While some Japanese Buddhist virtuosi (not to mention
the Buddha himself) sought for a nirvana beyond all magic, Buddhist
temples are as active as Shinto shrines in the purveying of amulets,
charms, and wonders.[15] In part, this is due to the belief common

8. For men, the ages 24, 41, and 59 are thought to be inauspicious. For women,
the corresponding years are 18 and 32. During these years, people should take special
care of their health.

9. Here I must take issue with Robert Bellah who believes that in Japan, as in the
West, there was "a tendency toward rationalization on both philosophical and ethical
levels which went far in freeing the world of primitive magic" (*Tokugawa Religion*
[Boston: Beacon, 1957] 63). While individual religious leaders and philosophers can
indeed be quoted to this effect, there was much less tension between the Japanese elite
and folk traditions over magic than there was in the West.

10. Reinhard Bendix, *Max Weber: An Intellectual Portrait* (Garden City, N.Y.:
Anchor, 1960) 93–94.

11. Winston Davis, *Dojo: Magic and Exorcism in Modern Japan* (Stanford: Stanford University Press, 1980) 211.

12. Ibid., 296.

13. For more on the rise of secular trends in Japan, see my "The Secularization of
Japanese Religion: Measuring the Myth and the Reality," *Transitions and Transforma-
tions in the History of Religions: Essays in Honor of Joseph M. Kitagawa* (ed. Frank E.
Reynolds and Theodore M. Ludwig; Leiden: E. J. Brill, 1980) 261–85.

14. Davis, *Dojo*, passim.

15. In the *Kevaddha Sutta*, the Buddha says, "It is because I perceive danger in
the practice of mystic wonders that I loathe, and abhor, and am ashamed thereof"

throughout the Far East that the dead, if not properly worshiped, will return to this world to haunt their descendants and to cause all sorts of mischief—sickness, poverty, bad luck, and even death. On the other hand, ancestral spirits will magically reward those who practice filial piety with good crops, a prosperous business, health and long life. Buddhism transformed traditional soteriological practices aiming at nirvana or better rebirths in the *next* world into magical techniques to ensure good luck (or apotropaic magic to ward off bad luck) in *this* world. For the masses of the Far East, Buddhism's doctrine of "skillful means" (Japanese: *hōben*) legitimated the use of chants and spells (*kaji-kitō*) that would heal their diseases and bring them material abundance. For example, some Buddhists call upon Amida Buddha for salvation (a practice called *nembutsu*). But the same words (*namu Amida Butsu*) can be used as spells (*dharani*; Japanese: *ju*) to drive out evil spirits. To put "teeth" into their prayers, rebellious peasants in Tokugawa Japan sometimes wrapped a long rope around a temple, shrine, or an image of Jizō and would threaten to pull the building or statue down if their demands were not met. Sometimes they promised to build the god a new shrine if he answered their prayers.[16] In some Japanese temples, priests continue to practice archaic healing rites deeply rooted in Japan's folk religion.[17] All of these practices suggest the importance, indeed the centrality, of magic in Japanese religion.

Japanese Buddhism has leaned towards the miraculous from the beginning. According to the story in the *Nihongi*, Buddhism was initially recommended to the Japanese court by the king of Pekche in Korea virtually as a form of magic:

> Imagine a man in possession of treasures to his heart's content, so that he might satisfy all his wishes in proportion as he used them. Thus it is with the treasure of this wonderful doctrine. Every prayer is fulfilled and naught is wanting.[18]

Early Japanese Buddhists used the new faith for practical ends. If the emperor became sick, hundreds of young people were forced to

---

(D.N., i, 213). Strictly speaking, Buddhist karma might seem incompatible with the popular notion of luck. But here we are talking about a popular tradition and about popular religious institutions which are more concerned about the ritualizing of optimism (and their own survival) than they are about logical consistency.

16. Nakura Tetsuzo, "Kinsei no shinkō to ikki," *Ikki* (ed. Aoki Michio et al.; Tokyo: Tōkyō Daigaku Shuppankai, 1981), vol. 4, *Seikatsu, bunka, shisō,* 304–5.

17. For good examples, see Carmen Blacker, *The Catalpa Bow: A Study of Shamanistic Practices in Japan* (London: Allen and Unwin, 1975).

18. *Nihongi: Chronicles of Japan from the Earliest Times to A.D. 697* (trans. William George Aston; Rutland, Vt.: Tuttle, 1972), 2: 66.

take monastic vows, as though the Buddha were an angry god who needed to be appeased! Sutras were recited "to bring rain, to stop pestilences of smallpox, leprosy or other epidemics and to avert the evil consequences of bad omens such as eclipses, comets, etc."[19] During the Nara period, Buddhism was thought to be such a powerful source of magic that monks were forbidden to teach the *dharma* to the people. Buddhist magic and religion thus became the monopoly of the state itself. Shinto-oriented lay bureaucrats and the *vinaya* itself (a set of monastic rules) carefully regulated the thaumaturgical powers of the monk. Monks could be returned to secular life for practicing divination or for using non-Buddhist spells to cure the sick. Witchcraft and black magic were proscribed by the rules of the sangha as violations of the rule of "right livelihood."[20] During the middle ages, after the religion successfully broke out of the fetters imposed by the court and spread among the common people, the founders of temples and sects routinely offered their services "for the protection of the nation," a move that blended magic, national sentiment, and self-interest at a single stroke.

A distinction should be made here between institutions which cater to the luck of the individual (e.g., prayer-temples and pilgrimage sites) and those which legitimate and dignify the family, the local community, and the nation, bringing the group itself good luck (e.g., the Shinto parish, Buddhist family temples, and religious institutions associated with the imperial family). This contrast roughly parallels the distinction between "motivated conduct" (in which religious affiliations are initiated "in order to" achieve some miraculous boon) and "obligatory conduct" (in which people are motivated to participate in religious activities or institutions "because of" the boons they have already received).[21] In general, "motivated conduct" is established "in order to" secure the good luck of the *individual,* while "obligatory conduct" is connected with institutions which underwrite the good luck of the *family* or the *community* itself. However, obligatory religious affiliations can also be used by individuals as an opportunity to advance their own luck. For example, while the festival of the Shinto parish aims at the revitalization of the community as a whole, individuals can also pray to the *ujigami* (clan gods) for their own health and happiness. Looked at from this perspective, the

19. Bellah, *Tokugawa Religion*, 67.
20. Hirakawa Akira, "Nihon Bukkyō no kyōdanteki tokushoku," *Bukkyō no shakaiteki kinō ni kansuru kisōteki kenkyū: Nihon Bukkyō o chūshin to shite* (ed. Furuta Sokin; Tokyo: Sōbunsha, 1977) 120.
21. See my "Japanese Religious Affiliations: Motives and Obligations," *Sociological Analysis* 44 (1983) 131–46.

temple or shrine can be thought of as a permanent magico-religious "marketplace" where human beings exchange gifts of food, prayer, and praise in return for material and/or spiritual "good luck." The following diagram (elaborated in Part II of this paper) summarizes these relationships.[22]

	Religious Affiliations and "Luck"	Related Forms of "Luck" (or Magic)
motivated conduct	1. *Ad hoc* relations with shrines, temples, shamans, fortune-tellers, etc. 2. New Religions	Individual luck dominant
obligatory conduct	1. Buddhist family temple 2. Shinto parish 3. Shinto parish guild	Group or community luck dominant; secondary use by individuals

Today, nearly every Buddhist temple and Shinto shrine large enough to sport a full-time office and staff sells amulets of one sort or another. Amuletic magic is especially obvious in "prayer temples" (*kitō-dera*) which, unlike "family temples," have no permanent congregation (*danka*) to support them financially. Prayer temples have therefore developed a variety of magical practices designed to ensure good luck in this world as well as in the next, and thereby their own well-being. The Buddhas they enshrine are usually "functional deities" specializing in the healing of a particular disease. For example, at the Narita Fudōsan temple, rites combining the rituals of wandering ascetics (*yamabushi*) and Esoteric Buddhism attract thousands of Japanese who want to ensure (or magically insure) the "traffic safety" of their new Nissans and Toyotas.

Two other examples will suffice as illustrations of the function of contemporary Buddhist temples as distribution centers for magic and good luck. Since 1960, a number of temples have appeared throughout the country called Sudden Death Temples (*pokkuri-dera*). These temples sponsor pilgrimages which cater to the needs of a population

---

22. For a complete statement of my position (and its relationship to sociological exchange theory), see "Japanese Religious Affiliations," especially figure 1: "Obligations, Motives and Religious Institutions," p. 142.

in which the proportion of elderly individuals increases every year. The Kichidenji temple in Nara is a good example of a Sudden Death Temple. Pilgrims are expected to visit the temple three times. On the first visit, they pray for long life and good health (i.e., general good luck). On the second, they pray for protection against accidents (i.e., more good luck). On their final pilgrimage, they return to the Sudden Death Temple to pray for an easy and quick death and for rebirth in Amida Buddha's Pure Land (*anraku ōjō*).[23] Pilgrims are invited to bring some of their underwear with them to be blessed by the priest (in the name of a toilet deity). This blessing allegedly will protect the elderly from *shimo no byō*, i.e., loss of sphincter control and other disorders of the "lower parts."

Another example of the temple as a purveyor and improver of luck is the cult of Mizuko Jizō. It is estimated that every year over a million Japanese women have abortions. Because people (including fetuses) who die violently are believed to take revenge on their malefactors, women who become ill after an abortion are apt to believe that they have been cursed. Many turn to Buddhist temples for help. A prayer distributed at the Shiun Jizō temple in Saitama prefecture declares: "Young spirits abandoned as fetuses, wandering in the darkness, bring tears to our eyes. They are crying out with all their might, 'Father help me, Mother help me,' but their yearning does not become a voice." Exploiting the guilt, fear, and superstition of these women, temple advertisements warn that the unappeased spirit of an aborted fetus can cause "cancer, heart disease, eye disorder, back pain, breast cancer, shooting pains in the arms, epilepsy, neuroses in youths, rebellion against parents, suicide." To avoid cancer (etc.) and improve their luck, women are told to worship Jizō, a Buddha who looks after children who have died *in utero* (*mizuko* literally means 'water children'). By dedicating a statue of Jizō, or by making a contribution to the temple, the infant's spirit can be appeased and the guilt can be lifted from the shoulders of its erstwhile mother. About two thousand Mizuko Jizō temples now offer their magico-religious services to women tormented by the spirits of their aborted babies.[24]

What, then, are the functions of temples and shrines in Japan? I can summarize what I have been trying to say thus far by stating

23. In such cases, one wonders whether final enlightenment (*ōjō*) can be distinguished from good luck itself. Indeed, reaching the safe harbor of heaven seems to be the ultimate form of good luck in most of the world's so-called great religions (and great magics), not just Japan's.

24. Tom Ashbrook, "Japanese Fight Guilt of Abortion," *Austin American-Stateman*, Aug. 31, 1985, p. C-12.

perhaps somewhat boldly—but realistically—that the phenomenological heart of popular religious activities is the quest for good luck, magic and a quick and easy way to enlightenment. In addition to these basic and unadorned functions, temples and shrines also have important latent functions. Among these is the one considered by functionalists to be the very raison d'être of religion: the unification of society. The best way to approach the unifying function of temples and shrines is to see *how* people are actually attached to, or affiliated, with them. In Part II, I shall discuss briefly the social structures of "clan" temples and shrines, Shinto parishes and parish guilds, confraternities, family temples, and the so-called New Religions. After this, we shall turn to more advanced forms of religious integration, i.e., civil religion and the "spiritual education" given by Japanese companies to their employees. In Part III, we shall look at the opposite function of religion, its disruptive role in society.

The Unifying Function of Temples and Shrines

Looked at from a broad, historical perspective, religious affiliations often begin as exclusive, monopolistic groups which, under the pressure of social and economic competition, evolve into more inclusive organizations. Shinto offers some of the best examples. In ancient Japan, Shinto worship was the prerogative of clansmen (*ujibito*), i.e., members of a specific clan (*uji*). It was forbidden even to look at the rites of another clan, let alone participate in them. The leaders of the clans (*uji-no-kami*) routinely served as clan priests, establishing the 'unity of government and religion' (*saisei-itchi*) as Japan's most archaic political principle. Even after these warlords were transformed into the civil nobility of the Yamato confederation, they continued to leave the court twice a year and return home to preside over the festivals of their clan god (*ujigami*). The taboos which the *ujigami* imposed upon the clan gave each a unique identity.

In the middle ages, clan gods and clan Buddhas (*ujibutsu*) continued to be worshiped in clan shrines and clan temples (*ujidera*) by clans of aristocrats and warriors. With the military turbulence of the fifteenth and sixteenth centuries, and the growth of an economy based on money and markets, the monopoly which older clans and families had enjoyed in sacred and secular affairs began to crumble. "New families" (the *nouveaux riches* of the countryside) rose to prominence. Temples and shrines once controlled by clans fell into the hands of the local folk.[25] In some parts of Western Japan, conservative Shinto

---

25. These local temples and shrines were known as *sonji* and *machidō*.

parish guilds (*miyaza*) were formed. By and large they were defensive
organizations established by "old families" which felt that power was
slipping out of their hands. Where there was a parish guild, only
members of select guild families could hold ritual positions. They,
and they alone, could make offerings before the gods or act as priests
and oblationers. In this way, parish guilds shored up social status by
transforming it into a religious monopoly, i.e., into institutions which
excluded competition and affirmed status just as the secular, economic
guilds (*za*) did.[26] As time went on, the same forces that destroyed the
exclusive clan temples and shrines began to erode the privileges of the
miyaza itself. Guilds were forced to admit to their membership some
of the up-and-coming families. In other cases, local rivalries resulted
in the formation of two or more guilds in the same village, e.g., an
"Upper" and a "Lower Guild." In the end, however, so many families
were enfranchised that the guilds became synonymous with the inclusive territorial parish itself, the *ujiko* (lit., the children of the clan),
or at least with a more egalitarian lay leadership. Thus, through a
process of "expanding enclosures," most monopolistic parish guilds
were transformed into the territorial Shinto parish of the present day.

During the Tokugawa period (1603–1868), as commoners became
more prosperous they became increasingly aware of their own family
identity. In imitation of the warrior elite, they installed Buddhist
family altars (*butsudan*) in their homes and raised large stone monuments over their family graves.[27] Gradually, the remaining clan
temples of the middle ages gave way to family temples (*dannadera* or
bodaiji) dominated by commoners. Not long after this, the shogunate
realized that these family temples were a convenient way to control
the masses. All families were forced to register with a specific
dannadera, thus proving they were not followers of Christianity (regarded by the government as the vanguard of Western imperialism).
In this way, Buddhism, which essentially is a universal, missionary
religion, was forced into the mold of a "natural" religion (J. Wach) in
which religious and civil identities became nearly identical. Affiliation
with a Buddhist temple was established not by the choice of the living
(as it had been earlier in Japanese history), but by the location of the
ancestral graves of one's family. As territorial and kinship identities

26. In Japan, as in the West, secular guilds had religious aspects—meeting, feasting, and signing contracts in the presence of their patron deities.

27. Likewise in the West, at the time of the Protestant Reformation (and the rise
of the middle classes) individual gravestones began to replace the single wooden cross
raised over all the graves in the churchyard. Previous to the rise of the "middle classes,"
a common grave had been the lot of the common man in Japan as in Europe.

supplanted personal commitment, the temple became firmly grafted into the stock of the local community.

Buddhist confraternities (*kō*, or *kōshū*) tended to develop in an opposite direction from the *miyaza*. They often began as "voluntary associations" formed in order to deepen faith in a particular Buddha (usually Amida). Some, such as the Shinto Koshin fraternities, also functioned as mutual aid societies. By the time it reached its second or third generation, however, the confraternity usually was transformed into a supplementary ritual obligation for the family. In contemporary Japan, many *kō* actually function as senior citizens clubs.

We turn now to the modern period. The so-called New Religions of the nineteenth and twentieth centuries broke into the life of the local community as bearers of adventitious deities, i.e., the kami and Buddhas from the world beyond the village. In a sense they are nothing new since they combine such archaic elements as shamanism, faith healing, Confucian ethics, Buddhist deities, and even biblical symbolism. Bound by tradition and by their countryside locations, Buddhist temples and Shinto shrines, could not keep pace with the "modernization process." In particular, they could not keep up with the physical and spiritual movement of the population as it moved from the countryside to the cities. Traditional temples and shrines were hard put to explain the misery caused by the fluctuations of the business cycle, by war, and political and social instability. Unlike Shinto, the New Religions had founders, usually shamanistic or charismatic leaders claiming to have had revelatory experiences and/or healing powers. What was genuinely new about these groups was their ability to "package" traditional elements in a way that appealed to modern men and women. This included an adroit manipulation of the mass media and an all-embracing regimentation which appealed to the faithful. It has often been pointed out that these groups have been especially successful in those sections of the Japanese working class not protected by large companies or labor unions. My own research in this area has shown that at least in the case of Sūkyō Mahikari, one of the more rapidly growing New Religions, members seem to have been largely drawn from the country's Tory proletariat.[28] While the social message of the new messiahs was nearly as ambiguous as the teachings of the older faiths, thousands were convinced by their adroit blending of miracles and platitudes. The institutions they established were (at least initially) "voluntary associations" and therefore more goal-directed (*zweckrational* as Weber would put it) than the

28. Davis, *Dojo*, 261-71.

old temples and shrines. The New Religions have therefore proven to be far more dynamic and flexible than the traditional religions. From a sociological point of view, what seems to be most interesting about these groups is: 1) they are living proof of how *wrong* Durkheim was when he declared that there are "no churches of magic," for in most cases their magic (or miracles) far excels that of the temples and shrines, and 2) they are a clear indication that Weber was *totally wrong* when he said that magic and religion are incompatible with industrialization. The New Religions make use of the material and cultural "contradictions of capitalism" in order to "prove" the truth of their gospels, and contrariwise, their gospels and miracles enable the faithful to cope with the modern world *as it is*. Ironically, there seems to be an "elective affinity" between the magic of the New Religions and the "functional rationality" of industrial society.[29]

We have seen that the unification of religion and government (*saisei-itchi*) was one of Japan's earliest political ideals. In ancient Japan, this ideal focused attention on an emperor or empress who until the time of the Taika Reform (A.D. 645) often doubled as a shaman or shamaness. After that time, they began to play a more restrained and respectable role as high priests of the indigenous Shinto faith. During the Nara period, Buddhist temples were placed under the control of the state. Bureaucratic functionaries (generally Shinto laymen) largely controlled the lives of the monks and even determined whether or not they were truly enlightened. To become a monk, to beg, to leave the monastery to perform austerities in the mountains, all required permission from the government. Monks could not build unauthorized chapels, engage in commerce, or money lending. They could not accept slaves, horses, cows, or weapons from their followers. They could be expelled from their orders for living outside official, urban monasteries, for fighting, being intoxicated, or preaching to the masses. By providing monks with food, clothing and shelter (i.e., the temple or monastery itself), the state was able to regulate every move of the monastic community. It thereby prevented the *sangha* from becoming an independent economic or political power—in addition to the religio-magical force it already was.[30]

Robert Bellah has argued that because of the "great pluralism of sects," institutional religion itself has not been a "major integrating mechanism" in Japanese society. Unfortunately, Bellah seems to measure Japan's social solidarity using a Western scale. Until modern times, the political unity of most Western countries rested upon the

29. Ibid., "The Cunning of Magic and Reason," 291–302.
30. Akira, "Nihon Bukkyō no kyōdanteki tokushoku," 103–26.

monotheistic premise "one Lord, one faith, one baptism." I would contend that syncretistic politico-religious systems behave differently. In societies of this sort, political and social unity is assured by the *overlapping of multiple religious affiliations.*[31] Each family is bound to the whole by or through its obligations to particular religious (and secular) institutions.[32] I call syncretism of this sort "centripital cultural differentiation."[33] Its unifying social effect can be seen only *when one looks at it as a total religious system.* Nevertheless, Bellah is certainly correct when he singles out the family and the nation itself as the the country's most powerful "religious collectivities."[34] We turn to this next.

The unifying role of temples and shrines—and the *saisei-itchi* ideal—was most important in the period after the Meiji restoration of 1868. While Western scholarship has generally called the religious force behind the modern Japanese state "State Shinto" or "Shinto Nationalism," the imperial cult went far beyond Shinto and included nearly every religious group in the country, with the exception of a few zealous adherents of Nichiren Buddhism, some (not many) Protestant sectarians, and members of the Japanese Communist Party.[35] When the Meiji oligarchs began to look for a religious

31. This is the principal sociological reason why exclusive, "single practice" sects such as Nichiren and True Pure Land Buddhism, Christianity, and some of the New Religions have caused such turbulence. They reject the division of the population into multiple religious affiliations, i.e., the centripital sectarian differentiation which has been the traditional symbolic focus for the integration of society.

32. Thus, when we talk about the unifying function of religion, we should not think of religion as an invisible, sociological "glue." Rather, it achieves its "ends" indirectly and unconsciously through people's daily activities and obligations. Even in our own society, society is "unified" by the various interlocking roles that bind individuals to their work, to clubs, civic groups, voluntary associations, churches, etc.

33. To avoid any confusion between religious pluralism and syncretism—the former being a distinguishing mark of "modern" societies—I call pluralism "centrifugal differentiation" and syncretism "centripital differentiation." See my *Toward Modernity: A Developmental Typology of Popular Religious Affiliations in Japan* (Ithaca: Cornell University East Asia Papers, No. 12, 1977) 33–35, 88–89.

34. Again, it is unfortunate that Bellah characterizes this as "mechanical solidarity," a Durkheimian phrase which brings to mind primitive societies. While the cultural templates of the Japanese before 1945—especially the imperial "system" itself—may have been an undifferentiated, primitive morass to the Western mind, the simultaneous development of a highly differentiated industrial society in the same country makes it impossible to use the term "mechanical solidarity." What we see in Japan during this period is rather a complex society culturally unified by the archaic symbologies of family, clan, land, and sacred kingship.

35. See Daniel C. Holtom, *Modern Japan and Shinto Nationalism* (Chicago: University of Chicago, 1943), and *The National Faith of Japan* (New York: Dutton, 1938).

platform for the Restoration, only Shinto seemed a likely candidate. Buddhism was too closely associated with the Tokugawa regime. Confucianism was too bookish and deficient in cultic appeal. Christianity was a minority religion, the object of popular fear and discrimination. Accordingly, the oligarchy decided to create a new politico-religious ideal based on a revival of the ancient system of government called *ritsu-ryō*. In 1868 a Department of Shinto was set up. At the same time, the government began to take steps to separate Shinto from its syncretistic ties with Buddhism. This finally led to the persecution and destruction of Buddhism in many provinces (the *haibutsu kishaku* movement of 1868–1871). The government then appointed Shinto and Buddhist priests, Confucian scholars, actors, professional raconteurs and even fortune-tellers to act as the propagandists of a new patriotic cult. But artificially concocted religions seldom catch on, and this was no exception. When the propagandists preached to the people, "members of the audience, when not observed, occasionally stuck out their tongues or ridiculed the sermons."[36] By 1871–1872 a turning point was reached. The popular reaction to the persecution of Buddhism convinced the government that national unity was being jeopardized by relying on an explicitly Shinto cult. In 1872, a system of national priests was established. In the following year they were given a set of revealing but nebulous doctrines to proclaim: respect for the gods and love for Japan, "heavenly reason" and the "way of humanity," respect for the Emperor and obedience to authorities. The new national faith was simply known as the Great Religion (*Daikyō*). But even this experiment was dominated by Shintoists, and probably failed for that reason. It was dissolved in 1875.

From about 1897, Shinto publication began to stress the "nonreligious" nature of Shinto shrines, the so-called *jinja-hi-shūkyō-setsu*. This obviously was a way to get around the contradiction between the freedom of religion guaranteed in the Constitution of 1889 and the *de facto* recognition and support given to Shinto by the government. In 1899, the Department of Education in its Order No. 12 forbade the teaching of religion in Japanese schools, while insisting that State Shinto was not a religion. Since neither the propagandists nor the national priests had been effective, the government was now willing to settle for a state religion whose priests were forbidden to preach. The result was a mute cult whose significance was revealed by Imperial Rescripts and by the orders of the Department of Education.

36. Kishimoto Hideo, *Japanese Religion in the Meiji Era* (Tokyo: Toyo Bunko, 1969) 133–34.

If public schools in America have served as a *de facto* established religion, in Japan they became catechetical institutes of the state cult.[37] They allowed the government to give the appearance of upholding freedom of religion while in fact supporting a state religion in both schools and shrines. In this way, the government could support a Shinto cult without seeming to detract from Buddhism, Confucianism, or Christianity. After years of trial and error, the new "non-religious" state cult seemed to be a solution to Japan's quest for a unifying spiritual center. Ironically, by neutering and depoliticizing Shinto, the state made it a more powerful tool of political manipulation.[38]

When we look at the confluence of religion and nationalism as a whole, it appears that the system of non-religious shrines was only part of a much more complex whole. Buddhists, Shintoists, and members of the so-called New Religions supported the Imperial Way with a zeal matched only by naivete. Japanese Christians, with some prodding by the thought control police, also got on the imperial bandwagon. A priest serving a Japanese Anglican church (which stands in the shadow of Tokyo Tower to this day) went so far as to identify the mystical "National Essence" (*kokutai*) with the Kingdom of God. Other Christians defended their faith as:

> the faithful mongoose that killed the communist viper; it was the devoted watchdog that kept away the burglar of radicalism; it was the guardian angel that protected the citadel of the national life against the demons of unsocial license. It inspired a true religious faith that brought the blessings of God upon the soldiers that faced ungodly forces across the Siberian border.[39]

The actual relationship between religion and Japanese nationalism can only be understood in terms of the *total system* of institutional and parainstitutional religion which sociologists nowadays call "civil religion."

In the civil religion of modern Japan, temples and shrines played a role similar to that of churches and synagogues in the American civil religion. They were the institutional anchors of a broad and diffuse network of ideas, emotions, and ritual behavior. By manipulating civil religious sentiment, oligarchs, militarists, and industrialists were able to convince the Japanese people that they were members of one

---

37. Sidney Mead, *The Lively Experiment* (New York: Harper, 1963) 68.
38. See Murakami Shigeyoshi, *Nihon hyakunen no shūkyō: haibutsu kishaku kara Sōka Gakkai made* (Tokyo: Kōdansha, 1968) 85.
39. Holtom, *Modern Japan and Shinto Nationalism*, 84.

national village, an extended family (*dōzoku*) or even distant members of the imperial family itself. By their adroit manipulation of the primordial symbols of kith and kin, they forged the imperial myth of stability and solidarity—the myth of a transhistorical, eternal dynasty. This myth was cleverly designed to contrast in a positive way with the constant change of dynasties in China, to create the illusion of continuity in the face of unprecedented social changes, and to beautify the exploitation of the lower classes both in peace and in war.

After the Pacific War, many of the symbols, self-images, and themes of the civil religion (previously anchored in temples and shrines) reemerged in the ethnocentric mythologies of the New Religions, in the "spiritual education" which industry gives to its employees, and in the journalistic and academic movement called Japan.Theory.[40] For years, many of the New Religions had proclaimed the racial superiority of the Japanese, the sacrality of the imperial family, and had even assigned Japan a central place in the creation of the world. They also encouraged their followers to work hard and subordinate themselves to the state. One of the post-war New Religions, Sūkyō Mahikari, teaches that the world was originally ruled by the Japanese emperor—then living on the "Continent of Mu"—and that in the "Holy Twenty-First Century" his rule will be reestablished.

Without indulging in such obvious ethnocentrism, the "spiritual education" (*seishin kyōiku*) given by Japanese firms to their employees has taken up some of the same themes. Throughout the country, companies sponsor flower arranging lessons, Zen meditation, paramilitary training on Self-Defense Force bases, and quasi-religious retreats for their workers in temples and other religious communities. Spiritual education seeks to instill in the working class such traditional values as diligence, loyalty, and self-denial. For example, many companies in Kansai send their young blue-collar workers to the Ittōen community in Kyoto to be taught that they should devote themselves selflessly to the firm, and that "money is not necessary"—

---

40. Japan Theory (*Nihonron*) or the Japanese Culture Theory (*Nihonjin Bunkaron*) is really not a "theory" at all. It is simply an outpouring of essays, books, and articles dealing with the old question "Who are we?" Contemporary Japan Theory is largely the product of culture shock—the traumata Japanese tourists, businessmen, and academics suffer when they leave the Hobbit-like comforts of home for the strange and disturbing world abroad. In recent years, the Theory has also assumed the role of defending Japan against Western criticism, especially against American charges of "economic nationalism" and "a free ride in defense." Japan Theory is anything but a primitive "effervescence" of religious solidarity. Rather, it is the quest for self-identity in the context of an international environment which has become uncomfortably complex. Religion plays a minor role in this literature, serving primarily as an example of the uniqueness of Japanese culture, not as its source.

religious ideals any company would be happy to promote! To drive the point home in the most dramatic way possible, workers who go on such retreats are expected to participate in quasi-sacramental toilet cleaning expeditions throughout the region in order to "lose their egos."[41] One is tempted to say that in modern Japan the firm itself has taken over many of the "transactional" functions of the traditional temple or shrine, just as the state did in the years before 1945.

Temples and Shrines as Sources of Friction and Disunity

The facts of Japanese history do not lend much credence to the popular Japanese conviction that theirs is a society uniquely based on harmony, cooperation, and mutual good-will. While Tokyo and other Japanese cities may be among the safest in the world, the most remarkable thing about Japanese society is not the absence of discord, but the difficulty the Japanese have in dealing with it once it has erupted. Hence their herculean struggles to avoid all sources of friction, their great reluctance to confront offenders head-on, and their remarkable endurance of violence and political tyranny. *These* are the characteristics that justly win for Japan the sobriquet of the "harmony society"—not just her achievement of social tranquility—commendable as it may be.

We should never let the Durkheimian or functionalist emphasis on religion's unifying role blind us to the *disruptive* potential of temples, shrines, and other religious institutions. When religion creates new groups out of other older ones it inevitably is forced to play a fissiparous social role. Because in unifying the new it disrupts the old, religious renewal contributes *both* to the maintenance of social solidarity *and* to the creation of tension, conflict, and disruption. While Westerners generally associate dyspeptic sectarians with religion's disruptive role, movements within churches and "mainline denominations" fall under the same sociological rule. The same is true in Japan where nearly every religious group or movement has been, at one time or another, rife with factionalism. Indeed, it is a rare religion which has seen no *coup d'église*. Religious splinter groups are seldom based on theology or matters of principle. More often they are the outcome of petty rivalries, personal allegiances, questions of succession, or petulant claims to unique religious revelations or magical techniques. Because social unity was traditionally predicated on the recognition of syncretistic affiliations ("centripetal religious

41. Davis, "Ittōen: The Myths and Rituals of Liminality," *History of Religions* 14 (1974-75) 282-321; 15 (1975-76) 1-33.

differentiation"), the appearance of "single practices" in the Buddhism of the Middle Ages—claims that there was only one way to salvation— often resulted in nasty controversies. The founders of the new Kamakura sects—men such as Eisai, Dōgen, Hōnen, Shinran, and above all, the irrepressible Nichiren—were no strangers to the bitter conflicts of this samsaric world. Other examples of religious rivalry might include the constant bickering between and within Buddhist and Shinto sects in the Middle Ages—including outright warfare between warrior-monks (*sōhei*) attached to the more powerful, landholding temples—the *Ikkō-ikki* and *Hokke-ikki* uprisings of the Pure Land and Nichiren sects during the fifteenth and sixteenth centuries, peasant rebellions inspired by faith in Maitreya (Japanese: Miroku) Buddha or other deities, tension between the state and Catholicism, Protestantism, and New Religions such as Ōmoto-kyō, Tenri-kyō, Sōka Gakkai, Tenshō Kōtai Jingū-kyō, or with Buddhism itself (e.g., the *haibutsu-kishaku* movement mentioned above), and internal struggles within the leadership of many sects, including the contemporary squabbles in Pure Land's Higashi Honganji, the Izumo Grand Shrine, and in the United Church of Christ in Japan (Nihon Kirisuto Kyōdan).[42]

Conclusion

In this essay, I have argued that 1) temples and shrines can best be understood as permanent institutions for worship, 2) the purpose of worship is, generally, the securing of good luck or magical boons, 3) temples and shrines therefore function as "marketplaces" where vows, prayer, and offerings can be exchanged for boons, and where "sacrifices of praise and thanksgiving" can be offered up for boons already received. We have seen that associated with each temple and shrine are religious associations acting to secure divine benefits for various groups within the community. While these affiliations have changed markedly in the course of history, temples and shrines continue to ply their ancient trade.

Japanese temples and shrines have helped to transmit to the industrial society of the present the wishful-thinking of primitive magic, pre-modern values, a feudalistic social ethic, and a form of "organic statism." Today, Japanese industry rests not only on the

---

42. For the tension caused by pilgrimage in the Tokugawa period, see my essay, "Pilgrimage and World Renewal: A Study of Religion and Social Values in Tokugawa Japan," *History of Religions* 23 (1983–84) 97–116 (Part I), 197–221 (Part II). For the recent struggle within the United Church of Christ in Japan, see my "The Cross and the Cudgel: The Ordeals of a Japanese Church," *Religion* 5 (1985) 339–71.

spirit of delayed gratification represented by Ishida Baigan, Ninomiya Sontoku, Suzuki Shōsan, and other traditional heroes of Japan's "work ethic." Contrary to the expectations of Max Weber, we have seen that modern capitalism in Japan has taken full advantage of the opportunities created by the magical *Geist* of the country's temples and shrines. Although Weber predicted that such an "ethos" would lead to stagnation, Japan has become the most successful form of managed capitalism in the world today. While temples and shrines continue to function as purveyors of good luck, they do not seem to be a direct contradiction of this industrial rationalism and asceticism. On the contrary, the temples and shrines of Japan suggest there is (*pace* Weber!) an ironic compatibility between magic and the "spirit" of the modern world.

The Temple in Image and Reality

David M. Knipe

IN BOOK XI OF THE *Metamorphoses* of Apuleius we find Lucius caught up in ecstatic adoration of the goddess Isis, gazing intently into her face, living within the temple precinct in order to continue the "ineffable pleasure" she instills in him.

> Every morning Lucius is the first one there, waiting for the temple doors to open. The white curtains have hardly been pulled aside from the statue of Isis before he, with the other worshippers, is invoking her. But when the others depart, he remains, contemplating the goddess in sweet peace of soul, meditating and keeping exemplary silence the whole day long.

With this summary of Apuleius by A. J. Festugière (1954: 81) compare a description by Robert Paul (1978: 135, 139) of a scene in the first floor of a Sherpa temple in northeastern Nepal.

> In turning away from the daylight of the outside world, one does not enter a void but (once the eyes are accustomed to the light) a seemingly chaotic plethora of images, symbols, colors, a profusion of symbolic forms certainly evocative of a dreamer, or a waking dreamer, a hallucinator or a psychotic. . . . It is a world of throbbing life, violent color and action, magical power, sex, and fearful aggression intimately linked in the cannibalistic and destructive *yab-yum* deities. . . . [The] village *lamas* sit and read texts invoking the aid of gods and also attempt actually to visualize the gods standing before them and finally merging with them. While this is going on, to the accompaniment of the eerie sound of the *lama* orchestra—bass drum, hand drum made from two skulls, cymbals, thigh bone trumpets, conch shells, flageolets, and huge alpine horns—and in an atmosphere pervaded by smoke and the odor of incense, women and laymen come and go, children dash around madly playing cockfight or hopscotch, and an occasional pious villager or someone in mourning performs an endless series of complete prostrations in atonement before the altar of the gods. The feeling is of swarming, buzzing confusion.

Two disparate sources, thousands of miles and years apart, one novelistic and perhaps autobiographical, the other anthropological, one "inside" and the other "outside," both concerned with a mysterious space containing symbols and devotees as well as mundane construction materials. Although some may argue that these two sources have little or nothing to do with one another, I submit that such mysterious space is our phenomenon, the topic of our symposium.

The phenomenon of "the temple" exists as remembered, ruinous, or reconstructed architecture, or as functioning structures of wood, stone, or steel. The temple exists, too, as a significant structure established in the cultural experience of some but certainly not all human societies, and is thereby an entity that challenges us with its complexity, diverse guises, and seemingly endless range of meanings.

The conference essays collected in this volume are by specialists in four areas of the ancient world (Sumer, Israel, Greece, and Mesoamerica) and two areas of Asia in which ancient temple traditions continue today (India and Japan). Obviously this is selective discussion of a widespread phenomenon that is labeled, with varying degrees of certainty, hesitation, or convenience, "the temple." Other specialists working in other areas, and in chronologies ranging from prehistory to the living present, might well have contributed historical and theoretical perspectives substantially different from those offered here.

What can we say about the temple from the broad and comparative perspective of the history of religions? What is the temple in image and reality, the alternate reality constructed by the believers, worshippers, and faithful whose structures, both physical and metaphysical, are the subject of this symposium? Our discussion must allow for multiple levels of meaning, some of them overtly declared in the significations of temple-building communities, others not at all obvious but hidden beneath or within apparent levels of meaning. No direct literal meaning of a temple will serve us crossculturally; comparatively speaking, we must start with the indirect meaning, the temple as symbolic construction, and proceed from there to examples from particular worldviews and the religious expressions of particular peoples in certain periods and locales. As scholars we may be at times wide of the mark in the attempt to decipher the temple-as-symbol-system in Eighteenth-dynasty Egypt or Tang-dynasty China. But then we confess, too, an inability to list and relate exhaustively all possible meanings a temple holds for Balinese Hindus today. Outside of the Eighteenth or the Tang dynasties we may be intrigued by the comparative historical venture into recognizing certain essential human experiences that, if not universal, are evidently transhistorical. The essays presented in this symposium invite comparative reflection that may illuminate the parts as well as the whole.

Let us consider temple creations, temple creators, and the worlds of meaning they declare, and do this from selected perspectives. First, there are the obvious approaches through considerations of sacred space and sacred time. Then again, temples may be studied through cultural perceptions of the body human and the body social. Further, we may perceive temples as expressions of tradition, as tangible extensions of intangible cultural legacies. Finally, we may uncover some of the opaque or hidden meanings and messages that temples bear in religious imaginations, some of them intended for insiders, others for outsiders.

In the comparative endeavor we are outsiders attempting to peer inside temples past and present. There are limitations neither on the number of temples available for us to study, nor upon our interpretations of what these constructions signify. And points of contrast between examples we may choose to consider are certainly not lacking.

Spaces, Centers, Passages

Concepts of sacred space are complex and varied: temples, shrines, sanctuaries, and altars are but a few of the participating components in kaleidoscopic symbol systems that may embrace every aspect of the physical world as well as every dimension of human consciousness. But the basic contours of religious expressions of space may become discernible, just as the Chinese landscape becomes featured and discrete to the eye of the *fengshui* specialist locating the correct and harmonious situation for a shrine or temple. A process of selection is apparent, as was recognized in the 1930s by the Dutch historian of religions, Gerardus van der Leeuw (1938: 2. 393): "Parts of space . . . become 'positions' by being 'selected' from the vast extensity of the world." Certain localities become positions by "the effects of power repeating themselves there, or being repeated by man."

Mircea Eliade adhered to this interpretation by van der Leeuw, but chose to speak of hierophanies, manifestations of the sacred. "A sacred place is what it is because of the permanent nature of the hierophany that first consecrated it . . . There, in *that* place, the hierophany repeats itself . . ." (1958: 368). Inherent links are thus declared between sacred space and sacred time. Furthermore, according to Eliade, the construction of every altar, temple or sanctuary is based upon a "primeval revelation which disclosed the archetype of the sacred space *in illo tempore*" (1958: 371-72). Often that revelation includes the notion of a celestial prototype, just as the city itself may be fashioned after an extraterrestrial mythic paradigm.

Eliade proceeded from this basic premise to explore three aspects of sacred space immediately relevant to our discussion of temples, as they are relevant, of course, to the study of altars, shrines, sanctuaries, ceremonial centers, and the houses, villages, towns, cities, or territories in which these are erected. One aspect is that of cosmogonic repetition: to construct a temple is to repeat the creation of the world. A second point is the symbolism of the center: the temple as reconstructed world proclaims the center of that world and integrates the components of that world. "If it is to *last*, if it is to be *real*, [it] must be projected by means of the construction ritual into the 'center of the universe'" (1958: 373). The third insight that Eliade provides for us is that the temple, like the sacred palace, town, or city, is assimilated to an axis mundi and a sacred mountain, a point of junction between heaven, earth, and the netherworld (1958: 375). This junction is one of communication and passage, and therefore of sacred transformation. (For Eliade's further discussion of sacred space see also Eliade 1954: 6ff.; 1959: 20ff.; 1961: 27ff.)

The most important contribution on sacred space since Eliade's is the prodigious comparative effort of Paul Wheatley, *The Pivot of the Four Quarters*, a study of the origins and diffusion of urbanism in ancient China and, in the second half of the work, a comparative study of ceremonial centers in ancient urban cultures across the five continents. Expanding upon Eliade's studies, as well as the astrobiological theories of René Berthelot (1949), Wheatley's "cosmo-magical" approach to symbolism for the comparative study of the center, the axis mundi, orientation, micro-macrocosmic correspondences, geomancy, and related subjects, has been influential on the scholarship of the 1970s and 1980s in both ancient and living traditions.

Earlier, numerous other scholars contributed toward definitions of sacred space, including Paul Mus (1935), who revealed to Western scholars the complex symbolism of Borobudur, a vast human-made mountain that is at once altar, temple, *maṇḍala*, *stūpa*, labyrinth, axis mundi, center of the world, body of the Buddha, and word of the Buddha. Stella Kramrisch (1946) investigated multiple aspects of spatial and temporal symbolism in the traditions of Hindu temple building, including the temple as *maṇḍala*, and Guiseppe Tucci (1961) further opened up the Indo-Tibetan symbolism of the *maṇḍala* and the methods of reintegrating cosmic space and time in a compact mystical diagram that may involve temples and deities as well as the human body, the palace, or the city as cosmic reference. Elsewhere, Vincent Scully (1979) linked the details of sacred geographies and symbols in his discussions of 150 Greek temple sites. Others have also enriched our understanding of this human need to found, integrate, and order space, and to allow for divine-human interaction in a sacred area or complex. (For additional studies see the references in Wheatley 1971 and Brereton 1986 with annotated bibliography.)

Our symposium presents further opportunities for discussion, as in the description by Samuel Noah Kramer of the temple of Enlil, the Ekur, known as the center of the universe, erected in the city of Nippur where heaven and earth are united, and assigned to the god in the cosmogonic moment. Thus, in this example from the history of Sumerian religion, the most powerful deity and the most honored temple are linked at the center of the world *in illo tempore.*

By contrast, Walter Burkert reminds us that not all temple traditions provide such tidy paradigms. Except for the complex at Delphi, navel of the earth, the Greek temple was neither center of the world nor axis mundi. Nevertheless, many Greek temples were dominant structures located at the centers of their cities, or upon commanding heights. For example, there is the temple of Athena Parthenos on the Athens' acropolis, or her Lindos temple set dramatically on the heights of the island of Rhodes, or the temple of Poseidon overlooking the sea from Cape Sounion.

Indeed, the construction of shrines and temples on the tops of hills and mountains is of worldwide occurrence, from the Punic temple of Tanit on the Byrsa of Carthage, to Mons Capitolinus, the hill with its temple of Jupiter that served Rome as ceremonial center and citadel from the sixth century B.C.E., to Mount Zion, the place where Yahweh dwelled, to Tai Shan, the Eastern Peak of Shantung province with at one time more than 250 Daoist shrines and temples, to the Miwa-jinja shrine that enables a worshipper to experience the immediate presence of the sacred Japanese peak. Throughout South and Southeast Asia, temples ritually constructed as mountains, as well as those on natural heights, are widespread.

The classic Mesoamerican temples described in this symposium by Gary Feinman were usually constructed singly or in pairs on truncated pyramidal mounds. Were these pyramids created as mountains? The unique Olmec "pyramid," built a millennium before the beginning of the classic cultures, belongs to the earliest phase of monumental construction in Mesoamerica. Erected at the center of the island of La Venta, without stairway, truncation, or capping enclosure, it rises from a circular base and displays deep grooves on the sides of its cone in the likeness of Los Tuxtlas volcanoes sixty miles away (Soustelle 1985: 33). Perhaps for the builders this established mountain was itself sufficient focus at the heart of the sacred complex, a mountain-as-image in a recreated world-as-temple. If so, its religious statement would resemble that of Hindus today who circumambulate the Arunacala (Dawn Mountain) of Tamil Nadu as if it were a temple (Eck 1986: 133).

Mountains, real or constructed, crags, cliffs, even unprepossessing hillocks rising from an otherwise flat landscape, all are liminal spaces denoting points of contact with celestial realms and their divine inhabitants or sacred powers. They are focal points for the divine-human encounter, for illumination, transformation, and passage. But then the opposite number to the mountain, the cave, has also served as sacred space and therefore as locus for sanctuaries, shrines, and temples. Consideration of the cave as natural sanctuary takes us to the other pole of the axis mundi and its point of access to the netherworld, again expressing liminality, passage, and transformation. The "religion of the caves" (cf. Eliade 1978–85: 1.16ff., citing André Leroi-Gourhan) involves us in conceptions established in certain regions more than 30,000 years ago, and the possibility of intricate symbolisms of maternity, gestation, and rebirth from the cave-womb, as well as initiatory and shamanic symbolisms of "ritualized quest" (cf. Burkert 1979: 90). Just as there are ritually constructed "mountains," so are there ritually constructed "caves," and we will return to the subject in part three of this essay.

Reintegration of space at the sacred center, orientation on the pathway of the sun (and therefore four walls in orientation), and a vertical axis that provides communication not only with celestial realms but also with subterranean worlds are among the foremost expressions of shrines and temples. When we consider this two-way path that is the cosmic axis, several dimensions of temple symbolism come into sharper focus. For example, my own current fieldwork in South India is concerned with a small temple in coastal Andhra that has grown up over a phenomenon commonly observed in India, an "anthill," that is, a termite or "white ant" mound that rises, like a mini-castle with several hardened turrets, well above ground level. This particular anthill, about five feet high, if excavated would also be found to descend into the ground as far as the termites needed to tunnel in order to tap water, in some cases as much as forty meters. In other words, it is a naturally emergent cosmic pole linking three worlds. As a hierophany yoked to certain pan-Indian motifs and symbols, the anthill is frequently associated with another axis, the endless *liṅga* or generative organ of the god Shiva, Lord of the dead, and further is considered to be the abode of serpents, also expressive of death and the powers of the netherworld, including rebirth. In the case of this particular temple that embraces the anthill as "image," the site functions as center for a vivid cult of regeneration and perpetuation of deceased children, particularly those who have undergone violent deaths, and serves as repository for *linga*-like "ash-fruits" molded by the Potter caste in the exact form of the anthill turrets to represent the dead.

This example reminds us that temples worldwide are sometimes also tombs and places of sacrifice not only to feed the deities, but to nourish ancestors as well. Tomb-shrines appear frequently in the paleolithic evidence, in caves with interiors painted red like a womb or in megalithic temples constructed in the shape of the womb (cf. Gimbutas 1986b: 337). In this regard, they are reminiscent of the living cult of Inari, the Japanese agricultural deity with uniquely red-painted shrines and mysterious entry-gates (Miller 1983: 302). In ancient Mesoamerica, the temple at Palenque was also a tomb, and the main axial street of the Aztec city of Teotihuacan, cosmically oriented, connected some 75 temples in a straight line of 2,000 meters and was the Street of the Dead. Sacrifice to the ancestors in Confucian temples is documented in the early fifth century B.C.E., and followed far earlier traditions. Concerning twentieth-century China, one anthropologist has reported from fieldwork in the 1940s in a village in the southwest the details of seances held in the temple for five days at the birthday of the Mother Goddess. Communications with the dead performed within a two- or three-year mourning period result in messages recorded by the priests in the temple record books, copies of which are taken home by devotees participating in the seances. In the history of Christianity the church altar as table, hearth, and tomb is well known (van der Leeuw 1938: 398; Brown 1981: 3, 9ff.). The Sherpa Lama's body lies in repose under the central shrine of the Nepali Buddhist temple mentioned above in the introduction (Paul 1978: 134).

Another dimension of sacred space that is illustrated in temple traditions both ancient and modern is that of refuge or "sanctuary": the notion of the sacred precinct as inviolable territory. Here again the perception of liminality, a place apart, is foremost. Illustrations of classical temples of the ancient Mediterranean world as places of refuge are well known, and a similar statement is made today by Christians in the United States who openly install refugees from the civil war in El Salvador in the "sanctuaries" of their churches. For another perspective on this notion of inviolability the sacred element of fire in ancient Iran provides an example. The Iranian temple whose architectural prototypes were established in the Achaemenid period, probably in the sixth century B.C.E., became the space to separate the fire from the world, protect it from death and corpses, from unconsecrated humans, even from the breath of its consecrated priestly servants, the only humans permitted to enter its closed chamber. If icons of deities such as the god Ahura Mazda, or the ubiquitous goddess Anahita, were in the temples at Pasargadae or Naqsh-i Rustem, or in their later variants built in the Parthian and Sassanian periods down to the Arab conquest, the sacred fire was nevertheless dominant (Wikander 1942: 33; 1946: 52ff.). The remnant Zoroastrian communities in India known as the Parsis still maintain rigorously this definition of sanctuary for the sacred element within their temples.

Finally, the most obvious of all aspects of sacred space-as-temple concerns the abode of the deity. Once again our phenomenon is subject to wide variation in the history of religions. Some temples are readily definable as the residences of a god or gods. The biblical temple, as Menahem Haran has indicated in our symposium, is clearly "the house of the Lord," a terrestrial palace in the mode of such divine residences known to the Sumerians, Akkadians, Canaanites, and other civilizations in the ancient Near East. But another meaning of the temple is disclosed in the remarkable open-air precincts of Bali in Indonesia. There one may find Hindu temples-without-walls in which great banyan trees sometimes dominate the rectangular, bordered sites, and huge upright stones, simply dressed menhirs, represent such Hindu gods as Vishnu, Brahma, and Shiva. That the deities are not residents but visitors drawn briefly to these menhirs for the offerings makes these open temples resemble the Polynesian *marae* (and possibly pre-Hindu Balinese megalithic sites) more than any Hindu prototype exported from South Asia (Lansing 1986: 346).

Time, Cycles, Histories

The temple complex or ceremonial center is for many cultures not only the reintegrated space of original creation but, as we have already noted, also the locus of original time, that is to say, the cosmogonic moment. As such the temple, the center spatially and temporally, is a cosmic resource. Time becomes encapsulated and portionable; it is ladled out routinely in the daily services of the temple and in megaportions during great festival occasions. The lives of the deities and the people are woven together in this sharing of the sacred time within the sacred space. No one could doubt such power when witnessing the daily procession of the Lord of Srirangam from his temple house to his rest house at 3 p.m. each day. It is accomplished through a sea of devotion from his people lining the main

street of the South Indian temple-town. And so we imagine the power
of the procession of Amun of Thebes down to the docks and then by
barque across the Nile to the West Bank every ten days, even as the
Amun of Karnak was carried down the long avenue of sphinxes once
a year to his Theban temple. The time segments of the gods are the
markers on the clocks and calendars of the people. And if the temple
as architectural chronometer is destroyed, as in the repeated case of
Jerusalem, it is not only spatial catastrophe but the meaning of time
itself that must be considered again from the top.

There is increasing documentation to support the notion that
ancient societies attained urbanization, and thereby more complex
and architecturally sophisticated sacred centers, during a process of
apprehending and declaring symbolically, ritually, and mythically the
correspondences between stated rhythms of celestial regions and those
of the biosphere, including the cyclical and interactive worlds of
plants, animals, and humans (cf. Berthelot 1949; Wheatley 1971: 414ff.).
Such a process may have accelerated markedly during the evolution
of plant-cultivating and animal-tending societies in the eighth, seventh,
and sixth millennia B.C.E. in western Asia, Eastern Europe, and
Thailand. The appearance of the first signs of agriculture in the
archeological record is followed closely by the appearance of shrines
or "proto-temples" in such sites as Jericho (ca. 7000 B.C.E.) and Çatal
Hüyük only a few centuries later on the Anatolian plateau.

To the cultivator, being responsible for a crop field, a life-
nurturing space, is being responsible as well for a new kind of tem-
porality, the crop time. The plant—wheat, rice, maize, cassava, beans,
etc.—exemplifies life that renews itself periodically (cf. Eliade 1958:
324–25; 1978–85, vol. 1:40–44; Grottanelli 1986: 141), and therefore the
mysteries of birth, death, and rebirth. Like its human cultivator (and
dependent), the plant undergoes a passage from seed to maturation to
harvest-cutting to rebirth. The maintenance of the seed of new birth,
the storage of the harvest, and the daily rendition of the harvest store
into food parts, and the food into human body parts, are all aspects of
these mysteries well documented in the history of religions. Shrines
and temples of early agrarian societies could not have been removed
from such mysteries and their constant concerns for sacred time. As
Marshack (1972) and others have opened to us the astonishing time-
reckoning powers of paleolithic humans, so too is the increasing
sophistication of ethnoarcheology revealing the complexity of eighth-
to-fifth-millennium B.C.E. agrarian life and worldview.

For example, some of the Old European civilization temples, or
small clay "models" of temples, contain storage jars, grinding stones,
and bread ovens, as well as feminine images and symbols. One
Ukrainian excavation of a site dated ca. 4700–4500 B.C.E. revealed a

seventy-square meter shrine centered on a large oven and female figurine; this Cucuteni (Tripolye) site contained 32 other schematically rendered feminine figurines, five of them seated at grinding stones (Gimbutas 1982: 72–73; 1986a: 513–14). In the scores of shrines excavated at Çatal Hüyük in southern Anatolia are hearths and ovens, and some shrines are physically connected to granaries. Grain offerings are plentiful. There is no evidence for animal sacrifice, although the dominant birth-giving goddess is constantly linked as mother and perhaps consort to the masculine bull and ram deities (Mellaart 1967: 77–130). Elsewhere in prehistoric evidence there is the excavation of the Anau (or Jeytun) culture of southern Turkmenia and a proto-temple cult center serving also as granary (Litvinskii 1986: 516).

In the historic civilizations on every continent there are many ties between public and domestic food storage and public and domestic temples and shrines. To cite examples from just two civilizations discussed in our symposium, two of the four temples discussed by Kramer were those of the goddess Inanna and the god Enlil. The Eanna, or "house of the date clusters (anna)" was the temple of the former, the "Lady of the date clusters." Jacobsen suggests that Inanna was originally the numen of the date crop at harvest time, and that "her range was early extended to that of the storehouse generally, including wool, meat, and grain" (1976: 135). And the result of Naramsin's destruction of the Ekur, temple of Enlil at Nippur, was the loss of grain for the people because grain was cut in the temple's 'Gate-in-Which-Grain-Must-Not-Be-Cut' (Jacobsen 1976: 16–17). A second illustration is from Japan. The great Ise national shrine, the most sacred precinct, is constructed in the manner of the ancient granaries. And the archaic cult of the agricultural deity, Inari, officially incorporated into national religious institutions in the seventh century, is still dominant in the Japanese religious landscape.

The accounting of time as "history" in the temple is thus apparent in the cult celebrations of the seasonal festivals and other passages. The reading of the Enuma Elish epic in the temple of Marduk on the Babylonian New Year's Day is a stock example known to every student of religions. There are worldwide parallels to this conjunction of the renewal of time, place, and devotion to the deity. But the temple records in its life and memory not only cosmic and divine events; it may also embody human experience, as for example in the deeds of heroes and kings, recited, like the cosmogonic deeds of Marduk, in the temple precinct, or dramatized by devotees taking the parts of ancient heroes. One regional oral epic of Andhra, South India, results in spontaneous possession, "death," and resurrection of devotees at the climax of an annual performance that may last for thirty nights in the vicinity of several historic temples (Roghair 1982). The temples mark the significant sites of the story that took place in the great time of the local warriors. And the enshrinement and ritual use in temples, sanctuaries, and churches of heroes' weapons, emblems, ships, even bones, is documented in ancient Greece, medieval Europe, India, Japan, and elsewhere (Knipe 1986a: 131).

We will return to the notion of the temple as cultural legacy in part five of this essay, but here let it be noted that the temple does indeed serve as a record of theophanies, as in the case of biblical and rabbinic literature accounting for the sanctity of Jerusalem and its temple (Haran 1978: 266–74; Levine 1986: 213; Smith 1978: 115–19), or to expand to the Hindu worldview, a record of hierophanies, for Hindu temples oblige the pilgrim with oral or sometimes interior inscriptional evidence of the mythic origins and events of the sacred place (cf. Shulman 1980: 17ff. on temple *sthalapurāṇas* and pilgrimages).

Temples may be seen to disclose time not only as solar, lunar, and seasonal passage, and as cosmic, divine, or heroic "history" but certain temples may also state the coincident perpetuation and cancellation of time, the cosmic ambiguity of change and permanence. This appears in the symbolism, for example, of Chinese temples even today: their floors and ceilings reveal the terrestrial/celestial cosmic axis in two mystical diagrams that are, like *yin/yang*, opposed but mutually dependent aspects of a cosmic unit. On the floor of the temple is the *lo-shu*, the earth chart, a square with 45 dots expressing change. Above the *lo-shu* in the rafters is the *ho-tu*, the heaven chart, a circle with 55 dots manifesting stability, while on the rooftop itself a red flowing pearl corresponds to the center dot of the *ho-tu's* concentric circular array of 55. That pearl-center is the cosmic point, the abode of the eternal, changeless Dao (Saso 1978: 401). The *ho-tu* (called the "river chart" because of its mythic origins as spots on a dragon-like horse emergent from the river) is linked by some traditions to the cluster of stars around the cosmic pole, the celestial constant, i.e., Ursa major, plus two esoteric stars that make up a magic square of nine (Saso 1978: 412–13). The Chinese temple is thus suspended between these two mystical, *maṇḍala*-like diagrams, both of them magic squares, both of them actively integrating speculations on the eight trigrams and five elemental phases that have been part of the Chinese worldview for more than two millennia. Not the least intriguing aspect of this symbol system that bonds micro and macrocosmic destinies in the locus of the temple is its versatility in the history of Chinese religions: this demonstration of change and permanence, of the ambiguity of cosmic time, is played out on many levels, in the classical Confucian scholars' preoccupation with history and the Yi Jing, the Book of Changes; in Daoist ahistorical philosophy as well as esoteric alchemical and talismanic expressions; in Buddhist cosmological notions; and in amalgamations and permutations at the popular religious level, including village temple rituals and symbols.

A parallel disclosure of mutability and immutability occurs in South Asian and Southeast Asian temples. To take Hinduism as an example, the great mountains of carved stone that are temples proclaim stability and a prehistoric resistance to time. And yet their architecture embodies temporal concepts. In this regard, as with sacred space, the temple perpetuates a part of the older Vedic heritage in which construction of the fire altar reassembled both spatial and temporal projections, the altar's 10,800 bricks in five courses, according to one tradition, representing the 10,800 hours (*muhūrta-*, 48 minutes each) in a year of five seasons. The classical Hindu temple observed the pole star above its center and axis, as it incorporated the symbolism of the lunar mansions (*nakṣatra-*) into its cosmic grid (Kramrisch 1946: 1. 72; Meister 1986: 372). The thirteenth-century Orissan temple of the Sun (Surya) at Konarak, designed to rise more than 200 feet, is a gigantic solar chariot of sculpted stone, the whole temple drawn on its twelve great wheels by eager horses, a million tons of stone in motion, and an apt simile for time, that passes yet endures. As with China, popular religious elements find means to insert themselves into traditional architecture: among the most frequented of interior acolyte shrines in many Hindu temples is one allocated for the worship of the nine planets (*navagraha-*).

In this way the temple in India becomes a sermon in stone, one heard by the Hindu or Jaina devotee whose personal passage through time (*saṃsāra*, the sequence of rebirths) is conjoined with the facts of divine and cosmic change and renewal (*pralaya*) displayed in the temple architecture, sculpture, and paintings. Change will occur in this life and in all imminent lives, as it does for the gods and this world itself, but the immutable Self, the one that resists change and transformation, is there all along and will rise through the roof of the body/temple/world to be like the pole star, eternal and changeless.

The periodic renewal of the temple building itself is another aspect of some temple traditions. Winston Davis has mentioned in our symposium the regular dismantling and rebuilding of the Ise shrine. This ritual, recurring every twenty years, involves the construction of an exact duplicate of cypress and thatch side by side with the old one, without alteration in material or technique since the seventh century. Feinman, too, noted Tozzi's hypothesis that certain Mesoamerican ceremonial centers may have been periodically renovated in connection with purification rituals. Templo Mayor, for example, was rebuilt or enlarged eleven times in two hundred years, about the same number of times as Ise in the same time frame, if not the same regimen. It may possibly be the case that in the highly conservative Mesoamerican examples, as in the Ise national shrine, a periodic return to the purity, cleanliness, and simplicity of beginnings is not only a demonstration of that continuity so precious to urban traditions, but also of the harmony that such a rhythm establishes between humans, sacred powers, and the cosmos in the shared time and space of the temple.

Finally, we might expand upon the paradox that temples account not only for prime time but for time out as well. Much of the power of Chinese Daoism, Japanese Shinto, and East Asian Buddhism in general derives from individuals with an inherent capacity to work the "in-betweenness" of existence, perform "actionless activity" (Chinese *wu-wei*) in the interstices of time and space made available only in sacred environments. Just as the temple or shrine may provide liminal space, so too may it identify a "gap" in time (Japanese *ma*, "interval" in space-time), a moment-out-of-moments in which reality may be apprehended and in which essential transformation may occur. In Japan the Buddhist awareness of the void, the essential emptiness of all things, was added to an innate allowance for the fleeting presence of multiple spiritual powers, the *kami*, and Japanese sacred architectural expressions capture superbly a "sensitivity to this atmosphere of ephemeral, temporary, spiritual presence." (See Pilgrim 1986: 140 for an excellent summary of the discussions of Arata Isozaki, Kisho Kurokawa, and others on *ma*, *kū* 'emptiness', *mu* 'nothingness', and other key terms.) Roman religion and sacred architecture are a far remove from the contemplative metaphysics of East Asia, but there too an interstitial time and space are identified in the temple. Janus, the gate personified and *numen* of the house door, god of beginnings, founder of the institution of sacrifice, is the embodiment of passage: one entering his uniquely constructed arch of a temple is neither here nor there, but literally and symbolically in passage (Rykwert 1976: 139–44).

Bodies Human

Among the most intriguing of the surviving structures of pre-history are the megalithic monuments of western Europe, including anthropomorphic tomb-shrines of the fourth millennium B.C.E., that is to say, constructed "caves" in the shape of human figures with stubby outstretched arms, not unlike the plans of cruciform cathedrals of Europe, as Gimbutas (1986b: 339, fig. 3) points out. Possibly they are themselves the Goddess, earth as Mother, the divine body as sanctuary and locus of collective rituals, as well as pregnant space for the deceased human body in the process of regeneration. And perhaps they carry the long paleolithic memory of the true cave habitat, the cave-womb deep in the model and prototype of all human females, the Great Mother, in whom deceased humans are returned finally to being.

This example of the womb reminds us of the prominence of the human body in sacred art and architecture, including the symbolism of temples. The "navel" of the earth, so frequently the definition of the sacred center, whether ka³ba or *stūpa* or Delphi, is another human body part, as is the male member, the *liṅga*, serving as center, axis mundi, imago dei, and altar in every Shiva temple and shrine of Hinduism. Temple symbolism may employ interlocking micro-macrocosmic correspondences, as we see in this metaphor from rabbinic Judaism, Midrash Tanhuma, Qedoshim 10:

> Just as the navel is found at the center of a human being, so the land of Israel is found at the center of the world . . . and it is the foundation of the world. Jerusalem is at the center of the land of Israel, the Temple is at the center of Jerusalem, the Holy of Holies is at the center of the Temple, the Ark is at the center of the Holy of Holies, and the Foundation Stone is in front of the Ark, which spot is the foundation of the world (Smith 1978: 112, citing A. Hertzberg).

An almost limitless supply of such metaphors and symbols is borrowed from the body and its functions. For over a thousand years before Hinduism began its temple-building era, the great Vedic Hindu sacrificial arenas were constructed on a scale taken from the measurements of the sacrificer's body. Standing with fingertips stretched up, the sacrificer provided a cord length that became a yardstick applied to the outlines of the altars and ritual enclosure on the great field of fire, a field representing at once the reintegration of universal space and time and the locus of regeneration for the sacrificer's new cosmic body (Staal 1983: 1. 195ff.). Space and time, subject to reintegration and regeneration via the human task of sacrifice, are themselves the projections of the divine sacrifice-person, Puruṣa-Prajāpati, whose cosmogonic self-sacrifice and dismemberment created the hierarchical three-world, three-fire, three-class system from his mouth, arms, and genitals/thighs, with a subordinate fourth social class, the serfs, created from his feet (Knipe 1975: 90ff.; 1986b: 476–77 and references).

Classical Hinduism perpetuated such human physiological (and sacrificial) templates in developing the canons for its sacred architecture from the fifth century c.e. The *garbhādhāna*, normally the impregnation ritual that concludes a marriage ceremony in the series of Hindu life-cycle rites, is performed upon the goddess Earth, and the seed of the temple is planted in her. The *garbha* is simultaneously seed, embryo, and womb; henceforth the completely "grown" temple will have as its sanctum a womb or liminal, generative space, the *garbhagṛha*. In this sense the temple is androgynous, since it is sometimes understood to be the unchanging masculine essence or spiritual presence, *puruṣa*, the unmanifest, in the midst of material manifestation and change, or *prakṛti*, the feminine. Since the temple is the body of the deity, the parts of the cosmogonically dispersed Puruṣa— the head with eyes and mouth, the neck, chest, legs—are all still to be found. So real is this divine architectonic body that the ceremony of consecration concludes with a ritual opening of the temple's eyes by means of a golden needle (Kramrisch 1946: 1. 67–97; 1983: 254ff.). However, unlike the disposable Vedic sacrificial arena, this classical Hindu temple is now a continuing entity in the human landscape, at once cosmic mountain with interior cave, body of the sacrificed god with interior womb, dwelling of the lord of this place with consecrated image, and mystical diagram incorporating all of the deities and all of space-time. If the Egyptian temple-builders borrowed stone to defeat time and describe eternity, their Hindu counterparts piled stone upon carved stone to display change: eternity is available neither to humans nor gods, but the unmanifest is captured inside the temple for all to encounter.

Buddhism too, from its early centuries in India to its periods of expansion throughout Asia, drew upon the symbolism of the body. In the first century B.C.E. in India the *stūpa*, a memorial structure often containing physical relics of the Buddha, was center of the world, axis mundi, and an integral ordered cosmos, i.e., the cosmic body of the Buddha. The *caitya* hall, a structure for community worship became an additional definition of sacred space in the same period. Shrines and temples were being constructed by Chinese Buddhists within three more centuries, by which time Indian Mahāyāna doctrines included the three-body worldview and the notion that the world itself is the lowest emanative body (and therefore temple) of the Buddha. The installation of larger-than-life images in the temples of India, China, Korea, Japan, and Southeast Asia, from the middle centuries of the first millennium C.E., allowed for additional architectural and symbolic expression. For example, the Sherpa temple of Nepal mentioned above in the introduction to this essay, has two floors and therefore two separate experiences for the worshipper, who encounters the head of the largest seated meditating figure, the bodhisattva Amitabha, protruding through the opening in the floor and dominating the space of the second story. As Paul indicates (1978:

139–40), the symbolism of this upper level of the divine body and temple represents "the triumph of the upper world, the sky, or spirit, over the underworld, earth, or matter." The head as locus of the event of release has a long history in all of the religions derived from South Asia.

As a third illustration from the history of religions we might recall as well the rich symbolism of Christian church architecture. The cruciform plan of the church is grounded as the crucified body of Christ. According to some traditions, if the choir does not lie in direct line with the nave, it is a reminder of the fundamental moment when the spirit of the God-man departed this world and his head sank to one side (Dahlby 1963: 55). The paradigmatic Christian sacrifice, the eucharist, is celebrated in the sanctum-head of the cruciform, oriented to the east, where the altar is a table for the dual offerings of food, blood and flesh transformed to wine and bread. This same space is also the tomb, as we have noted above, and once again we find an axis mundi connecting netherworld, human space, and heaven, illustrated in the frequent translation of the relics of saints and martyrs and their deposition under or inside of the altars of churches. The bones of the saints become one with the architectonic bones of the divine body in such a "privileged place" (cf. Brown 1981: 3, 9ff.).

We could continue with the important traditions of the interiorization of sacrifice and the manner in which a living human body becomes a shrine or temple in motion. India provides examples of such in every phase of its history, and Christopher Fuller has mentioned one in our symposium, i.e., the *jangam-* of South India who wanders about as a living shrine. The Daoist master is another, quite different illustration within the framework of meditative rituals that result in the interiorization of every component of the world of sacred space and time (cf. Saso 1978: 413–14; Schipper 1978: 381). And we might also consider further the symbolism of above/below, inside/outside, and right/left in temple construction and detail, as for example, in the universal South Asian practice of circumambulating the temple and then, once inside, the image, with the auspicious right side toward the sacred center (cf. Lincoln 1986: 499–505, and Lipsey 1986: 505–11, and their references for discussions of body symbolism in general). The overall impression one gains from the study of the great temple traditions of antiquity, in the New World or the Old (the Mediterranean and west Asia) is the power of cosmic orientation and an architecture (although not an iconography) decidedly non-anthropomorphic. For some traditions, however, including the three living faiths we have cited, links between human and divine bodies (Puruṣa, the Buddha, Christ) are avowed in definitions of sacred space, as they appear to have been in the megalithic tomb-shrines constructed five or six thousand years ago. We see that it may not always be a distinction between "historic" and "cosmic" modes of reference that is the deciding factor in this range of symbolism.

Bodies Social

It is widely assumed that temple-building societies are sedentary ones with established agrarian bases, if not already urbanized then urbanizing, displaying complex hierarchical social structures, including priestly classes and ruling elites with royal courts providing patronage for cult activities on the part of the society, and, further, owning traditions of architecture, sculpture, painting, as well as of writing and the preservation of texts in libraries. Pastoral nomadic societies are not known for their temples, libraries, or life-size sculptural arts. The Vedic religion of ancient India clung to a deep heritage of mobile, livestock-breeding communities: their great sacrificial arenas, as we have seen, were complex structures of micro-macrocosmic correspondences requiring for the construction of an altar as much as a year of rituals and 10,800 consecrated bricks. But those arenas were (and still are, in the surviving Vedic-Hindu traditions of South India) disposable at the conclusion of the rituals, and their iconic traditions remained minimal throughout their heritage in South Asia.

Surprisingly, however, recent archeological efforts point to that same archaic pastoral legacy for our earliest record of ceremonial centers reflecting an Indo-European worldview. The Indo-Aryan experience on the Indian subcontinent began in the middle centuries of the second millennium B.C.E. and left us the earliest *literary* evidence, in the concluding book of the Ṛgveda, dated about the close of the millennium, for that distinctive mark of Indo-European tradition, a divine-social hierarchical tripartition. We must go to the steppes of Central Asia and the late second millennium B.C.E. to locate what might possibly be the earliest *architectural* expression of the cosmogonic division of the cosmos, the divine pantheon, and the human social classes, an expression that was destined to live on in various guises in thousands of ancient Iranian fire-temples and Vedic sacrificial arenas, as well as subsequent temples of Zoroastrianism, Hinduism, Buddhism, and Jainism. Dashly 3 (see Litvinskii 1986: 517 and Russian references) includes a 150-meter-square enclosure for a circular edifice containing nine towers and a number of fire altars. The intriguing feature of construction is the plan of three concentric circles within the square, perhaps a representation of the three divisions of the world/gods/people/fires according to the functions of divine sovereignty (heaven and its gods, priests, offering fire), warfare (midspace and its gods, warrior aristocracy, prophylactic fire), and production (earth and its gods and goddesses, the masses involved in livestock breeding and small farming, domestic fire). If this is indeed a construction of Indo-Iranian peoples this particular "sociocosmic model," with three rings within a square in maṇḍala-like plan, was retained architecturally neither on the Iranian plateau nor in northwest India, although of course both Avestan and Vedic texts provide ample documentation of a tripartite-within-quadrapartite society in cosmogonic hierarchy.

The temple as symbol of sociocosmic hierarchy is a familiar feature in the history of religions. Architecture becomes a physical expression, one more reinforcement of the manifold separation of the ranks of society according to function and status. The priestly and ruling classes are of high rank and therefore close proximity to the deity of the temple; the elite is destined for service. As a living example of priestly traditions we may cite the Zoroastrian temples in Bombay: the performance of the primary liturgy, the *yasna*, or fire sacrifice, with its recitations from the Yasna text, occurs five times daily within carefully marked boundary lines inside the temple. Only the consecrated priests may enter such a sacred precinct and perform these rituals that guarantee cosmic benefits for all people.

Our symposium has brought up illustrations of additional ways in which temples convey social and demographic distinctions and demarcations. Feinman has discussed Mesoamerican Teotihuacan in the classic era as a city with neighborhood temples, each of the more than two thousand apartment compounds of 60 to 100 persons containing at least one temple. And Fuller has noted the ways in which priestly specialists, the headmen, and devotees of deities, temples, and shrines specific to caste or clan groups, may cooperate in the performance of major temple festivals in South India. In southwestern village China in the 1940s clan temples were a significant dimension of social, ritual, and festival life. In one village of about one thousand households, or eight thousand people, twelve clan temples served those ancestors of the wider clan who were not included in the household shrines maintained by every individual family. The central hall of each temple contained three shrines for male and female ancestors, with the oldest ancestor, the clan patriarch, established in the center of the middle one (Hsu 1948: 50–53, 167–99). In this last pair of examples there are highly competitive, frequently hostile, social segments. But the social body which understands itself to be cosmogonically fragmented into ranked orders of beings among all the kinds of beings in the cosmos, finds itself a unity in the context of a single time and space and pantheon. So too has Christianity spoken, through its divisive history, of "the Church" as the single body of Christ, an indivisible physical and spiritual unity, an *ecclesia* of those "called out" from profane labors.

Thus while some temples were closed to the masses, as were some of the Mesoamerican sanctuaries atop pyramids (Gendrop 1986: 389), and others, like ancient Egyptian temples, conducted schedules of important rituals out of sight of the masses, still other temples gave expression to the incorporation of the people assembled for worship as the society in microcosm, organized in the presence of the deity.

Political and economic dimensions of temple traditions are also well known. According to Livy the first session of the Senate each year in Rome was in the temple of Jupiter Capitolinus, with the leaders of the city offering sacrifices and performing vows, appropriately enough, to the divine sovereign Jupiter (Dumézil 1970: 1. 287). The collective wealth of the people is frequently housed in the temple, the correct place for treasure, in the safekeeping of the deity and provider. Tirupati's temple of Śri Veṅkateśvara in Andhra is the best known example from India today of a collective repository symbolizing the beneficence of the god himself. Frequently the liminal space behind the altar or behind the images of the deities becomes the temple treasury, as in the case of the magnificent temple of Ramesses III at Medinet Habu on the West Bank at Thebes, where disguised doorways lead to small rooms for the treasury and secret cult objects, or the temple at Dendera with its eerie crypts beneath the sanctum of the goddess Hathor containing wealth and, more importantly, the *ba*-image, the spiritual Hathor, the provider goddess.

Traditions and Culture

We confront the structure of the temple, an edifice of wood, stone, textiles, ceramics, and possibly metals. It is the dwelling of the deity or deities, and its sacredness is their presence. Its sacredness is further embodied, as we have seen, in the symbolic expressions of the individual, in correspondences between divine and human form and function, and in representations of the community of the faithful. The sacred is also displayed in the temple as repository of culture and center of tradition. The temple is thus not only the space of the deity, service of the deity, worship, ritual, and festival, but frequently also the arena of music, dance, drama, poetry, education, and sometimes even medicine and healing. In this secondary or derivative sense the temple may then be recognized as gallery, museum, stage, forum, school, and laboratory, a center where the multiform traditions of a culture are conveyed from one generation to the next.

It is not unusual to find stored away, or openly revered in temples, certain statuary, paintings, or cult objects from a distant past, a remote dynasty, perhaps a previous civilization. An example is the recent find of a small, perfectly preserved Olmec jade mask carved two thousand years before it was deposited in front of Tlaloc's shrine at the Aztec Great Temple (Templo Mayor) (Carrasco 1982: 183). In the same way that iconography is preserved, the sacred text, the living word is cherished and maintained. If written, that word may be inscribed or painted into the temple architecture and decor. If oral, the temple will be the place of recitation and litany, and perhaps also of transmission from teacher to pupil, from one human keeper to another. If both written and oral texts are involved, as is the case with the Zoroastrian temple liturgy, with its single written text, the Vendidad, bracketed by oral recitations, then the word is perceived as multiform. In any case, the temple becomes a place of continuing revelation. Vedic mantras, for example, always recited, not to be read aloud, have a triple career within Hindu temples. First, the larger, more powerful deities command diversified staffs that may include a specialist trained in one or another branch of Vedic texts. At the proper points in the daily liturgy he will be called upon to recite in this ancient Indic precursor to Sanskrit; otherwise, the rituals proceed without him in Sanskrit and the local language of the people. Second, quite apart from the liturgical calendar of the priestly staff, and without any contact with entering devotees, Vedic specialists frequently use some corner of a temple for teaching, for the *guru*-to-pupil transmission of texts, a line at a time, over a period of several years until the text, or collection of texts, has been interiorized by the disciple. Third, a member of the priestly staff or, for that matter, an educated lay person, may wish to study printed books including Vedic texts and commentaries and do this for personal benefit and edification within the temple precinct.

Iconography in the service of temple tradition has limitless variation, from the terrifying vulture goddesses pecking at headless corpses in the seventh-millennium B.C.E. wall paintings of Çatal Hüyük, to the regal golden pumas in the Incas Temple of the Sun at Cuzco. The great *stūpa* of Borobudur is a pictorial display for the pilgrim devotee, a biography of the Buddha to be encountered by the worshippers panel by carved stone panel as they ascend the corridors level after level to the crown of the cosmic mountain. And the devotees standing in the second court of the mortuary temple of Ramesses III at Medinet Habu did not need to be there on the great processional days for the festivals of Min and Sokar and other great deities. Successive phases of the festivals are painted and incised in lifesize figures on the interior walls of the open court, just as features of the daily temple rituals are prominently displayed on the walls of the first court (cf. Murnane 1980: 21–39). The temple-as-icon is familiar all over India, as for example, in Khajuraho, where today a vast park of 20 temples, the survivors of 85 built there in the tenth and eleventh centuries, stand as a panorama of Hindu mythology and medieval Indian culture, the dynamism of that age sensuously evident in every carved detail.

The temple precinct, complex, or compound as stage and school for religious drama, dance, and music is another well-known aspect of cultural transmission in temple-building societies. Connections between specific sites of sacred power and traditions of ritual dance and drama are at least as old as the paleolithic cave art depictions of masked dancers. And the shaman, as we know from historic examples of his or her techniques of ecstatic possession, exorcism, magical flight, and mastery of fire, is an artful performer, dancer, and raconteur, as well as ritualist. Virtually all of the living religions of Asia have perpetuated ritual dance and drama in multiple levels of popular and classical traditions, often with direct connections to shrines and temples and overt displays of shamanic sources. Hinduism, Buddhism in a great range of cultural manifestations, Daoism, and Shinto all provide abundant illustrations.

To take Hinduism as a specimen of temple dance and ritual drama, architectural features of the medieval North Indian temples began in the eighth century c.e. to include a dance pavilion (*naṭamaṇḍapa*) as an essential component along the main axis of the structure. This building in which the deity was entertained had its counterpart in courtyards or theaters for dramatic and dance performances in a tradition that predates the Common Era. Since Hindu deities such as Shiva, Krishna, Kali, and others are famous for their cosmic dances, it is not surprising that dance traditions were integral components of South Asian religions. The famous *devadāsis*, hereditary female "servants of the deity," included dancing as one of the traditional 64 arts preserved by them in temple service of the Lord. Performances of classical Sanskrit epics, or medieval plays based upon the epics and purāṇas (cycles of Rama and Krishna, for example), have long been prominent in connection with temple traditions in many parts of Southeast Asia as well as in their Indian homeland. And local or regional epic performances in one or

another of the vernaculars of India may go on for twenty or thirty
nights of performance and involve several temples and shrines in their
sacred geography (cf. Roghair 1982).

We have already mentioned the connections between the great
seasonal festivals, especially the New Year, and the temple traditions of
ancient Egypt, Greece, and the Near East. Theodor Gaster has made a
comparative summary of the emergence of ritual drama in the civilizations of the Egyptians, Mesopotamians, Hittites, and Canaanites, with
discussions also of literary survivals in biblical and classical Greek
poetry in his *Thespis* (1961; cf. also Gaster 1986). Deposition of the
reigning king, ceremonial marriage (*hieros gamos*), combat, and a
communal feast are among the principal components of a ritual
program that Gaster and others of the "myth and ritual" school have
identified (although not without controversy) as a characteristic pattern.
The Akitu festival, an annual drama of renewal in the temple of
Marduk during the first twelve days of the year, included the reading
of the epic Enuma Elish before Marduk's image, and the degradation,
then restoration, of the king of Babylon during the time in which the
year itself was regenerated.

The temple complex as school for the servants of the deity, from
priests and recitants to dancers, actors, and others, including the
kitchen staff whose labors feed the deity, is one aspect of education as a
cultural phenomenon. Another is the education of the public, or a
particular class within the society. In Confucian tradition it was for
more than two thousand years the scholar class that was the learned
elite at the top of the social hierarchy. The temple was the site of
instruction in the Confucian classics including history, philosophy,
ritual, poetry, and music. "Passage through the central front gate of the
Confucian temple was a symbol of the importance of classical learning,
a privilege traditionally reserved for successful civil-service candidates
of the highest rank" (Steinhardt 1986: 382; see also the plan of the
Chang-hua temple, including its Education Hall, White Sand College,
and Scholars' Residence). As a contrasting example, the Jaina tradition
of western India has an equally ancient, also still extant system of
education taking place in temple towns, but one that is open to all ages,
classes, and both sexes. It is during the rainy season that mendicant
monks and nuns are stationary, living in the peripheral rooms of Jaina
temples, never worshipping in the temple's inner chambers, since they
have transcended the life of lay rituals. Daily, however, they deliver
two-or three-hour sermons in temple assembly halls, expressing basic
teachings of the faith to large gatherings of the faithful, whose
continuing education is invariably enriched by these erudite and well-
traveled mentors.

Finally, there are traditions of healing associated with particular hierophanies, and therefore with shrines and temples that mark them, and these may be found in almost every culture and period up to the present day. The Hellenistic temples of Asklepios, god of healing, at Epidaurus and on the island of Cos (where Hippocrates established the science of medicine) look back to a long tradition of divine healing accomplished within a sacred precinct. Aristophanes' early fourth-century B.C.E. comedy Plutos (lines 620ff.) provides context for the central ritual in the cult of Asklepios, the "incubation" in which the devotee (in this instance Plutos, god of riches, who has been blinded) is put to bed in the temple precinct, where he experiences curative dreams and visions. Asklepios' temples at Epidaurus, Athens, Pergamum, Rome, and elsewhere became pilgrimage goals for those in search of healing, just as accounts of miraculous cures and exorcisms made the shrines of saints magnetic to pilgrims in late-antique Christianity (cf. Brown 1981: 113–20). Today, all over the Roman Catholic world, centers of healing are still to be found in great Marian shrines and churches such as Lourdes and the Basilica of the Virgin of Guadalupe in Mexico City. On the slope of the royal mount for which Montreal is named is the Oratory of St. Joseph, goal for nearly four million pilgrims a year. The interior walls of the stone church are festooned with thousands of crutches abandoned by the faithful after miraculous restorations at this holy place.

Shrines and temples in Japan, and the healers associated with them, are often disease- or problem-specific, as in the case of the "Splinter-pulling Buddha" in Koganji in Tokyo, or the 1400-year-old Nakayama temple from which pregnant women acquire white sashes to wrap over their stomachs, or another temple in the Nakayama complex that specializes in infants' illnesses. The Ishikiri shrine in Osaka has a venerable tradition of one hundred pilgrimages, the accomplished number bringing a hoped-for cure to one suffering from what would presumably be a lengthy illness (Ohnuki-Tierney, forthcoming).

Models, Meanings, and the Imagination

As a final segment in this essay let us consider the open-endedness of temple symbolism, as well as certain opaque or disguised expressions. We have already discussed a number of hidden meanings layered under apparent meanings, for example, in our overview of sacred space, the tomb is discovered as womb and site for community worship, and in another case, the altar as locus of death and sacrifice is revealed to be the table for food and life. In the discussion of temples and time we might have noted that certain temples act as physical calendars: when the sun's rays enter the sanctum it is the solstice, or the first day of the new year. And the deliberate destruction of temples, periodically, by their inside authorities rather than agonistic kin or expansionist neighbors, may indicate a mirror to the perceived pattern of cosmic renovation or a cultural penchant for the purity of beginnings, or both of these and yet again something else. There are so many symbol-facets of temples and areas illumined by them in the religious imagination to be considered. Some of these facets pertain to the temple as viewed by the insider, that is, the person of faith and belief within the community. Others concern the outsider's perspective, what that same temple may signify to the excluded or the stranger to the faith.

All that we have discussed with regard to temples thus far has concerned the enduring and affective presence of images derived from the experience of the sacred, images translated into an architecture and iconography that is substantial and always precisely separated from the unconsecrated world of profane substance. But we have by no means exhausted the possibilities of imaging the sacred. Temples are constructed not only in the scale of dwellings for larger-than-life deities, but also fashioned, both concretely and abstractly, in the realm of the imagination. They occupy, to borrow a phrase from Bachelard (1964: 184), "the space of elsewhere." Let us apply this space of elsewhere to the so-called "models" of temples mentioned above in part two, those discovered in excavations of the Old European civilization that existed from ca. 7000 to ca. 2000 B.C.E. in the area from the Aegean northward to the Danube and beyond, and from the Adriatic to Anatolia. Appearing in the archeological record from all parts of Old Europe, and from the sixth millennium B.C.E. on, these terracotta objects are striking in their variation and detail. They are considered by prehistorians to be models of existing temples, temple complexes, shrines, sanctuaries (the nomenclature is quite fluid) of communal use, and since they are frequently found in the vicinity of bench altars, some have been labeled "gifts to the goddess" (Gimbutas 1986a: 511-13; cf. 1980; 1982: 67-88; Dumitrescu 1968). Some are clearly miniature depictions of active shrines. One from Popudnia, Ukraine (Gimbutas 1982: fig. 23), contains miniversions of items found in full-scale shrines: a cross-shaped platform for votive offerings, a female figurine grinding grain, an oven, benches, vases, and another female holding her breasts. Others from Romania and Yugoslavia (Gimbutas 1982: fig. 21; 1986a: fig. 8) are rectangular structures topped by heads, human and bird: these could be interpreted as "stations" inside the shrines for the goddess as bird or pillar, respectively. The fact that tiny terracotta thrones, tables, and stools were modeled for shrine figurines in Ruse, Bulgaria, to cite one example (Gimbutas 1982: fig. 33), might support this view. Still another "model," one from the late fifth millennium B.C.E. discovered in 1966 in Cascioarele, Romania (Dumitrescu 1968: figs. 1–5), is widely discussed as a complex of four temples on a high platform (stereobate) or set of terraces. The four upper structures are uniform and on the same level, uncharacteristic of temples for typically hierarchic pantheons. They could be houses with ridgepoles, if not shrines, and thus a "village" or representative community set on a hill, or the many-leveled earth itself. Could this object be connected to a cult of the dead, possibly clan rather than family ancestors, with the many round apertures in the imposing chthonic base signifying cave-like tombs, and the total icon, a marvelous synthesis, replicating the goddess as womb-earth-tomb-house-shrine? The fact that the dead were buried under the floors of houses and shrines would be an essential clue. If my interpretation is correct then this is indeed a "temple complex" of great antiquity, but not one situated on the stereobate of Greek temples four thousand years later. It is a temple complex because it is first of all a tomb complex, and the horizontal lines on the icon are those of the Earth herself.

The important point for our discussion is the religious imagination and its capacity to engage with sacred space. Some of these small terracotta objects may be models of, and models for, actual buildings. Others may have been "temples" for spiritual occupation, by deity, devotee, or ancestor. The terracotta effigy jars excavated at Haçilar, Anatolia, and throughout Old Europe are sometimes in feminine form. One such hollow terracotta from Vadastra, Romania is identified by Gimbutas (1982: fig. 91) as a model of a temple "probably dedicated to either the Bird or the Snake Goddess." It has a complex labyrinth-facade and, incongruously, its own solution, a door ten centimeters high, directly at bottom center. This self-sufficient statement of the chthonic goddess offering rebirth from the difficult labor is a precious one (and is to recur much later in the Cretan mistress of the labyrinth, *potinija dapuritojo*). Such goddess-jars with multiple meanings are not unique in the history of religions, nor confined to antiquity: today the goddesses of India are represented in hundreds of rituals by the placing of a plain or decorated everyday pot on the ritual site.

These goddesses-as-shrines with doors or utilitarian openings invite us to consider the architecture of access. A set of correspondences between the cult house or shrine, the deity, the realm of the dead, and the deceased may have been widespread among archaic cultivators. The ethnological studies by Adolph Jensen reveal a striking illustration

that may be of interest to those seeking to interpret Old European
effigy jars or similar artifacts from the Mediterranean or West Asian
neolithic. In his chapter on the divine soul (1963: 283) Jensen discusses
primeval dema-deities and concludes that

> the dominant deity was the first to embark on the journey into death and
> to choose the land of the dead as his permanent abode. Thus Sido, the
> most important figure among the Kiwai of New Guinea, transforms
> himself into the house which represents the realm of the dead and which
> is duplicated in the cultic houses here on earth. In Western Ceram,
> Satene, the [female] ruler of primeval beings, exercises power in the
> land of the dead. Entrance into the land of the dead, then, means not
> only reunion with the ancestors but, especially, reunion with the deity.

To return to the historic ancient societies and what they express
in this architecture of access, the ancient Egyptians, who were also
fond of modeling for use in their vast necropoleis such things as tiny
tables and chairs, beds, barques, food items, even servants (*ushabti-*),
constructed false doors on their tombs and temples. It was the *ba*, the
bird-like ghost, who passed through the door of stone on the Old
Kingdom *mastaba*, the "most sacred spot in the funerary chapel,
where . . . the spirits welcome the king in their midst" (Frankfort 1948:
97). That liminal space between this world and the next had its
counterpart in the false door of certain Egyptian temples, directly
behind the deity's innermost shrine. Those not permitted access to the
god or goddess inside, for example, Hathor at Dendera, could be "in
touch" outside and, more important, could be heard in prayer by her
through this permeable stone.

The sense of sight is more the point in Hinduism where a similar
architectural access in spirit prevails. The *ghanadvāra* is the Indian
false door, "a door which is no door. No one can enter through it, but
the deity inside the temple has become manifest on the wall through
it" (Kramrisch 1983: 256, discussing the Aihole temple of Mahakutes-
varanatha, ca. 600 C.E.). And it remains true in Hinduism that the
devotee takes into himself or herself the "sight" (*darśan-*), the trans-
formative experience of seeing and being seen by the deity, or even
his or her temple from a long way off.

Entrance in spirit has no limit for the religious imagination. In
Bali today miniature shrines are a commonplace in crop fields, school-
rooms, craft shops, or standing on poles, like mail-boxes, in front of
homes. Some resemble houses, but they are not "models" of houses;
they are resting places for important spirits who receive their daily
offerings of food, flowers, incense. And in North India, to cite two

contrasting examples, low-caste village exorcists and healers fashion tiny *maṇḍapas* or "temples" from perishable materials not as seats or residences for deities but as traps for ghosts and demons to be removed from the person or house and burned, while "temples" three feet in height are constructed from sapling poles, leaves, and cloth by others, the Ahirs of Senapur, for example, in order to provide temporary snares for spiritual powers or tutelary spirits who then, in ritual circumstances, move to possess shaman-like specialists (Planalp 1956: 2. 805–17). Clearly, the "temples" in these three instances are quite different models from those discussed above; much of the difference, however, lies in the fact that we know their contexts. The two North Indian illustrations, one concerned with trapping, one with harboring delegations from the world of the spirits, reflect in part a recognition of demonstrable powers in the temples of a Hindu brahmanical elite and the appropriation of such powers by specialists of the sacred in particular initiatory or curative episodes and dramas.

The space of "elsewhere" rendered accessible to the spirit occurs in art forms never so vividly as in Chinese landscape paintings, sculpture, and calligraphy. There the model of the temple or shrine occurs once more, again with fresh conception if not total context. The Daoist artist condenses the world into paintings, or tiny objects of jade, soapstone, cork, or terracotta (see Rawson and Legeza 1973: pls. 1, 3–5, 12, 17, 26 for examples). The eye notes the upward flow of mountains, crags, pine trees, cloud formations, but only gradually does it appreciate, tucked in a crevice, at one with the other changing forms and growing like them, a temple. It is there at the point of merger of the celestial cloud-mountain, the *yin-yang* symbol of transcendence. The Daoist contemplative, a spiritual wanderer in the tradition of ancient sages and immortals such as Zhuang-zi (Chuang-tzu) in the fourth century B.C.E., voyaging shaman-like back to the origins of the world, does not always need to climb on pilgrimage to the temples on Tai Shan or other sacred peaks. He can insert his magical body and soul into such a mini cosmos, find the mountain-deity on which the temple, like its real-life counterpart, is merely a natural viewpoint or resting place, and proceed from within on his quest for the peak, heaven, immortality, imperishability. This soul-journey is possible because of the intricate correspondences between organs and dispositions of the human body and the cosmic elements, directions, and seasons, and the fact that transformation of all of these phases is natural to the Dao. The Daoist adept can in fact tell us his version of something we have observed in temple symbolism on several continents. As a free and easy wanderer in the mythical mountains and clouds the Daoist would-be immortal makes himself female, finds a cave-womb under the pole star, becomes simultaneously (like the devotee in the Hindu *garbhagṛha*, and perhaps, the worshipper in the megalithic tomb-shrine), mother, womb, embryo. He *is* the temple growing in the hidden crevice of the mystical mountain. And more, when the temple is superfluous, he *is* the space of elsewhere.

These considerations of space and an architecture of access lead us back to a recognition that all temples and shrines are, in a certain sense, models. They are symbols of power and presence. In some there is space for spiritual beings and the physical bodies of devotees as well; in others the space of the temple is just as accommodating but human corporeality is not a necessary ingredient in the divine encounter. Certain Hindu traditions might say it is the head, with all of its disinformation, that is superfluous: it is in the temple of the goddess that the determined devotee prostrates himself, according to a widespread genre of myth and folklore, there in ecstatic devotion to remove his head in ultimate offering. But the temple may also be a symbol of worldly power, that is, cosmic authority established on earth. The Ekur, temple of Enlil in Nippur, was a place that brought terror and dread into the hearts of foreigners and Sumerians as well, as Kramer noted in his symposium presentation. A trap or net for the workers of evil, it may have been a place of judgment and punishment. Temples can therefore stand in judgment and proclaim law, righteousness and order to outsider and insider alike. The massive pylons of Egyptian temples are such proclamations of power and of the capacity to defeat the minions of disorder. More than this, as Murnane has observed, "the Egyptians regarded their monuments as being charged with magical power, and the temple's facade is seen as a protective barrier" (1980: 20). Ramesses III (ca. 1182–1151 B.C.E.), to take an illustration of a type, is depicted on the initial pylon of Medinet Habu as a gigantic figure smiting down the enemy; he is king and deity expanding the cosmos, establishing order where chaos had ruled. The slaughter of the captives is a prominent motif on numerous temples, the victims' racial and ethnic features and dress apparent in telling detail as they are terminated, almost sacrificially, before the gods. If an onlooker were permitted as far as the first court's interior walls, he would be daunted by the graphic display of heaps of human testicles and hands, advertisements that the lineages of those who resist this divine sovereign will be fruitless, their bodies uncreative. Such models of cosmic power were of course well advertised in Mesoamerica when, for example, the Aztecs captured the human and material resources of the periphery of their world, then sacrificed or buried these treasures in the sacred center (Carrasco 1982: 182–83).

These sacrificial patterns in temples as emblems of power lead us to examine a final motif within the religious imagination: temples as models of transformation. The temple or temple area is the space of communication and therefore the space of sacrifice. The public cult of the Jerusalem temple, in the pattern of the ancient Near East, required daily sacrifices morning and evening. While prayer was optional, as Haran stressed in his presentation, sacrifice was usually the desideratum in temple service. Without sacrifice the fragile bonds between deity, humanity, and cosmos were not intact. And as Feinman noted in this symposium, the Aztecs assumed the awesome responsibility of maintaining cosmic existence by continued sacrifices, in or near the temple, of the "precious water" of human blood. And so it is with nearly every temple tradition we have discussed, one of the greatest mysteries of the history of religions is the drama in the precinct of the temple, the ritual killing, or a symbolic equivalent of that efficacious sacrificial death. Even the Jaina temples, filled with those whose spiritual ambition is eventual and total obedience to the doctrine of non-injury to living entities, reveal an obsession, *via negativa*, with the meaning and significance of killing.

The temple is the right space, as we have seen, to take on the meaning of death and transformation. Center of the world, beginning of time, abode of the receiving and giving deity, fount of revelation and tradition, this space is generative and true. And every temple tradition had, or has still, its schedule of revisions in both performance of, and speculation about, sacrifice, often in a trajectory of increased spiritualization and symbolic substitution (Knipe 1981). One of the most dramatic changes is well known: the destruction of the second Jerusalem temple. "The temple was thus turned into an eschatological symbol, to be resurrected only at the end of days . . ." (Haran). We see the temple in this example not only as unit of transformation for the self (Lucius in his Isis temple, moving in the grace of Isis from bestiality to divinity; the Sherpa devotees in their temple, destroying the world outside with all its dust of passion, in their long path to liberation) but also as model of transformation of an entire culture. In a sense the temple, space of sacrifice, becomes the sacrifice, becomes the symbol of absence, becomes the deconstructed space of elsewhere.

Reference List

(*ER=Encyclopedia of Religion*, ed. Mircea Eliade, 16 vols. New York: Macmillan, 1986.)

Bachelard, Gastón
    1964   *The Poetics of Space.* Boston: Beacon.

Berthelot, René
    1949   *La pensée de l'Asie et astrobiologie.* Paris: Payot.

Brereton, Joel P.
1986   Sacred Space. *ER* 12: 526–35.

Brown, Peter
1981   *The Cult of the Saints*. Chicago: University of Chicago.

Burkert, Walter
1979   *Structure and History in Greek Mythology and Ritual*. Berkeley:
        University of California.

Carrasco, David
1982   *Quetzalcoatl and the Irony of Empire*. Chicago: University of
        Chicago.

Dahlby, Frithiof
1963   *De heliga tecknens hemlighet: Symboler och attribut*. 5th ed.
        Stockholm: Diakonistyrelsens.

Dumézil, Georges
1970   *Archaic Roman Religion*, 2 vols. Chicago: University of Chicago.

Dumitrescu, Hortensia
1968   Un modèle de sanctuaire découvert dans la station énéolithique de
        Cascioarele. *Dacia* n.s. 12: 381–94.

Eck, Diana L.
1986   Mountains. *ER* 10: 130–34.

Eliade, Mircea
1954   *The Myth of the Eternal Return*. New York: Pantheon (also pub-
        lished under the title *Cosmos and History*).
1959   *The Sacred and the Profane*. New York: Harcourt Brace Jovanovich.
1958   *Patterns in Comparative Religion*. New York: Sheed and Ward.
1961   *Images and Symbols*. New York: Sheed and Ward.
1978–   *A History of Religious Ideas*, 3 vols. Chicago: University of
85   Chicago.

Festugière, André-Jean
1954   *Personal Religion among the Greeks*. Berkeley: University of
        California.

Frankfort, Henri
1948   *Kingship and the Gods*. Chicago: University of Chicago.

Gaster, Theodor H.
1961   *Thespis: Ritual, Myth, and Drama in the Ancient Near East*. Rev.
        ed. New York: Harper and Row.
1986   Ancient Near Eastern Ritual Drama. *ER* 4: 446–50.

Gendrop, Paul
1986   Mesoamerican Temples. *ER* 14: 388–90.

Gimbutas, Marija
1980   The Temples of Old Europe. *Archaeology* 33: 41–50.
1982   *The Goddesses and Gods of Old Europe*. Berkeley: University of
        California.

1986a   Prehistoric Religions: Old Europe. *ER* 11: 506–15.

1986b   Megalithic Religion: Prehistoric Evidence. *ER* 9: 336–44.

Grottanelli, Cristiano

1986   Agriculture. *ER* 1: 139–49.

Haran, Menahem

1978   *Temples and Temple-Service in Ancient Israel.* Oxford: Clarendon; reprinted Winona Lake, Ind.: Eisenbrauns, 1985.

Hsu, Francis L. K.

1948   *Under the Ancestors' Shadow: Kinship, Personality, and Social Mobility in Village China.* New York: Doubleday.

Jacobsen, Thorkild

1976   *The Treasures of Darkness: A History of Mesopotamian Religion.* New Haven: Yale University.

Jensen, Adolph E.

1963   *Myth and Cult among Primitive Peoples.* Chicago: University of Chicago.

Knipe, David M.

1975   *In the Image of Fire.* Delhi: Motilal Banarsidass.

1981   Sacrifice. Pp. 637–40 in *Abingdon Dictionary of Living Religions,* ed. Keith Crim. Nashville: Abingdon.

1986a   Epics. *ER* 5: 127–32.

1986b   Prajāpati. *ER* 11: 476–47.

Kramrisch, Stella

1946   *The Hindu Temple,* 2 vols. Calcutta: University of Calcutta.

1983   *Exploring India's Sacred Art,* ed. Barbara Stoler Miller. Philadelphia: University of Pennsylvania.

Lansing, J. Stephen

1986   Megalithic Religion: Historical Cultures. *ER* 9: 344–46.

Leeuw, Gerardus van der

1938   *Religion in Essence and Manifestation,* 2 vols. New York: Macmillan; reprinted New York: Harper and Row, 1967.

Levine, Baruch A

1986   Biblical Temple. *ER* 2: 202–17.

Lincoln, Bruce

1986   Human Body: Myths and Symbolism. *ER* 6: 499–505.

Lipsey, Roger

1986   Human Body: The Human Figure as a Religious Sign. *ER* 6: 505–11.

Litvinskii, B. A.

1986   Prehistoric Religions: The Eurasian Steppes and Inner Asia. *ER* 11: 516–22.

Marshack, Alexander

1972   *The Roots of Civilization: The Cognitive Beginnings of Man's First Art, Symbol and Notation.* New York: McGraw-Hill.

Meister, Michael W.
   1986   Hindu Temples. *ER* 14: 368–73.

Mellaart, James
   1967   *Çatal Hüyük: A Neolithic Town in Anatolia.* New York: McGraw-Hill.

Miller, Alan
   1983   Religions of China and Japan. Pp. 216–323 in *Religions of Asia*, by John Y. Fenton et al. New York: St. Martin's.

Murnane, William J.
   1980   *United with Eternity. A Concise Guide to the Monuments of Medinet Habu.* Chicago: Oriental Institute; Cairo: American University in Cairo.

Mus, Paul
   1935   *Barabudur: Esquisse d'une histoire du bouddhisme fondée sur la critique archéologique des textes*, 2 vols. Hanoi: Impr. d'Extrême-Orient.

Ohnuki-Tierney, Emiko
   Forth-   "Contemporary Japanese Religions in Health Care." In *Health and*
   coming *Medicine in the World Religious Traditions*, ed. Lawrence E. Sullivan. New York.

Paul, Robert A.
   1978   The Sherpa Temple as a Model of the Psyche. *American Ethnologist* 3: 131–46.

Pilgrim, Richard B.
   1986   Foundations for a Religio-Aesthetic Tradition in Japan. Pp. 138–54 in *Art, Creativity, and the Sacred*, ed. Diane Apostolos-Cappadona. New York: Crossroad.

Planalp, Jack M.
   1956   Religious Life and Values in a North Indian Village, 2 vols. Diss., Cornell University.

Roghair, Gene H.
   1982   *The Epic of Palnāḍu.* Oxford: Clarendon.

Rawson, Philip, and Laszlo Legeza
   1973   *Tao: The Chinese Philosophy of Time and Change.* London: Thames and Hudson.

Rykwert, Joseph
   1976   *The Idea of a Town: The Anthropology of Urban Form in Rome, Italy, and the Ancient World.* Princeton: Princeton University.

Saso, Michael
   1978   What is the Ho-t'u? *History of Religions* 17: 399–416.

Schipper, Kristofer
   1978   The Taoist Body. *History of Religions* 17: 355–86.

Scully, Vincent
  1979   *The Earth, the Temple, and the Gods: Greek Sacred Architecture.*
          Rev. ed. New Haven: Yale University.
Shulman David D.
  1980   *Tamil Temple Myths.* Princeton: Princeton University.
Smith, Jonathan Z.
  1978   *Map is not Territory.* Leiden: Brill.
Soustelle, Jacques
  1985   *The Olmecs: The Oldest Civilization in Mexico.* Norman: Uni-
          versity of Oklahoma.
Staal, Frits
  1983   *Agni: The Vedic Ritual of the Fire Altar,* 2 vols. Berkeley: Asian
          Humanities.
Steinhardt, Nancy Shatzmann
  1986   Taoist Temple Compounds and Confucian Temple Compounds.
          ER 14: 380-83.
Tucci, Guiseppe
  1961   *The Theory and Practice of the Mandala.* London: Rider.
Wheatley, Paul
  1971   *The Pivot of the Four Quarters: A Preliminary Enquiry into the
          Origins and Character of the Ancient Chinese City.* Chicago:
          Aldine.
Wikander, Stig
  1942   Gudinnan Anāhitā och den zoroastriska eldskulten. *Religion och
          bibel* 1: 26-48.
  1946   *Feuerpriester in Kleinasien und Iran.* Lund: Gleerup.

Additional Bibliography

Courtright, Paul B. "Shrines." *ER* 13: 299-302.
Davies, J. G. *Temples, Churches, and Mosques: A Guide to the Appreciation
    of Temple Architecture.* New York: Pilgrim, 1982.
_____. "Architecture." *ER* 1: 382-92.
Frankfort, Henri. *The Art and Architecture of the Ancient Orient.* New York:
    Penguin, 1969.
Fuller, Christopher J. *Servants of the Goddess: The Priests of a South Indian
    Temple.* Cambridge: Cambridge University, 1984.
Goodrich, Anne Swann. *The Peking Temple of the Eastern Peak.* Nagoya:
    Monumenta Serica, 1964.
Mabbett, I. W. "The Symbolism of Mount Meru." *History of Religions* 16
    (1983) 64-83.
Meister, Michael W., and Nancy Shatzman Steinhardt. "Buddhist Temple
    Compounds." *ER* 14: 373-80.

Müller, Werner. *Die heilige Stadt: Roma quadrata, himmlisches Jerusalem und die Mythe vom Weltnabel.* Stuttgart: Kohlhammer, 1961.

Patai, Raphael. *Man and Temple in Ancient Jewish Myth and Ritual,* 2d ed. New York: KTAV, 1967.

Steinhardt, Nancy Shatzmann (ed.) *Chinese Traditional Architecture.* New York: China Institute of America, 1984.

Tomlinson, R. A. "Ancient Near Eastern and Mediterranean Temples." *ER* 14: 383–88.

Turner, Harold W. *From Temple to Meeting House: The Phenomenology and Theology of Places of Worship.* The Hague: Mouton, 1979.

DATE DUE

DEC 17 '90			